ADORO TE DEVOTE

(St. Thomas Aquinas)

Devoutly I adore you, O hidden Deity
Who truly lie hidden under these figures
My whole heart subdues itself before you
For it finds itself wholly lost in contemplating you

Sight, touch, and taste are each deceived in you
But by hearing only can we safely believe
I believe whatever the Son of God has said
Nothing can be more true than this word of him who is the Truth

On the cross was hidden your divinity alone
Here your humanity also lies concealed
Nevertheless, believing and confessing both,
I pray for what the penitent thief prayed
(Lord, remember me, and take me into your kingdom)

Your wounds I do not see as Thomas did
Yet do I confess you to be my God
Make me evermore believe in you,
Put my hope in you and love you

O memorial of the Lord's death
O living bread offering life to human beings
Grant that I may live because of you
And always taste sweetness in you

Devout pelican, Lord Jesus,
Make me clean in your blood
One drop of which can save
The whole world from all sin

Jesus, whom veiled I now behold,
I pray let happen what I so thirst for
So that seeing you face to face
I may be happy in seeing your glory

Eucharistic Adoration in a Monstrance, courtesy of Wikimedia.org,
https://commons.wikimedia.org/wiki/File:Eucharistic_Adoration_-
_Monstrance.jpg

AT MASS WITH JESUS ON CALVARY

REFLECTIONS ON THE PRAYERS OF THE MASS AND THE REAL PRESENCE OF JESUS IN THE EUCHARIST

FR. GENE MARTENS, SJ

En Route Books and Media, LLC

St. Louis, MO

ENROUTE
Make the time

En Route Books and Media, LLC
5705 Rhodes Avenue
St. Louis, MO 63109

Imprimi Potest
Very Reverend Ronald A Mercier, SJ, Provincial
USA Central and Southern Province of the Society of Jesus

Imprimatur
In accordance with CIC 827, permission to publish has been granted on December 2, 2019, by the Most Reverend Mark S. Rivituso, Auxiliary Bishop, Archdiocese of St. Louis. Permission to publish is an indication that nothing contrary to Church teaching is contained in this particular work. It does not imply any endorsement of the opinions expressed in the publication, or a general endorsement of any author; nor is any liability assumed by this permission.

Cover credit: TJ Burdick from a photo taken at the Chapel of the North American Martyrs, White House Retreat, 700 Christopher Drive, St. Louis, MO 63129

Library of Congress Control Number: 2019951639
ISBN-13: 978-1-950108-56-5
ISBN-10: 1-950108-56-2

CONTENTS

Adoro te Devote – Prayer of St. Thomas Aquinas

FOREWORD

The Eucharist, we are told, is "the source and summit of the Christian life" (*Lumen gentium,* 11). It is more than a mere symbol. It constitutes the Church since it brings into our midst the salvific presence and action of Our Lord Jesus Christ. All the other sacraments point to and flow from it. It is the sacrament of sacraments, the mystery of mysteries. The quintessential prayer of Christ and his Church, it embraces three important terms: banquet, presence, and sacrifice. It is a sacred meal that both makes present and foreshadows the heavenly banquet. It brings the presence of the Risen Lord into our midst by transforming bread and wine into his body and blood. It makes present and immerses us in Christ's sacrificial death on Calvary. Without it, the Church would not survive, let alone exist. Christ's mystical body cannot exist apart from the saving mysteries present in the sacrament of his body and blood: in it "the whole Christ is truly, really, and substantially contained" (CCC 1374).

Given the centrality of the Eucharist for the Catholic faith, it is disturbing to learn from a recent survey of the Pew Research Center that less than a third of U.S. Catholics believe that during Mass the bread and wine actually become the body and blood of Christ. Even if allowances are made for the way the questions were asked and for what those polled understood to be the official teaching of the Church, the lack of understanding of the Catholic teaching on the Real Presence among U. S. Catholics is a matter of grave concern and calls for renewed efforts to explain this central truth of the faith. The likelihood that the percentage of those who believe in the Real Presence (and those who do not) has not substantially changed in recent decades makes the need for better catechesis all the more urgent.

In his book, *At Mass with Jesus on Calvary: Reflections on the Prayers of the Mass and the Real Presence of Jesus in the Eucharist*, Fr. Gene Martens, S.J., provides a helpful response to this pressing need. Using ordinary language and insightful metaphors, he offers a valuable resource for explaining the doctrine of the Real Presence to today's believers and explains what happens at Mass in a way that can be easily understood by the average Catholic in the pew. His presentation of the theology of the Eucharist and his careful commentary on the Eucharistic Prayers provide sound catechesis without watering down or oversimplifying this great mystery of the faith. If it is true that "the law of prayer [is] the law of belief" (*lex orandi, lex credendi*), then Fr. Martens has rendered us an invaluable service by showing us how the prayers of the Mass reveal the Church's deepest and most fundamental beliefs about the Eucharist.

–Rev. Dennis J. Billy, C.Ss.R., author of *The Meaning of the Eucharist: Voices from the Twentieth Century* (En Route Books and Media, 2019)

PREFACE

One day back around 1970, while teaching freshman religion at Rockhurst High School in Kansas City, Missouri, I asked the students in my class what they remembered about their First Holy Communion. One student raised his hand and said, "I was trying to figure out how you squeeze a man into that tiny piece of bread!" The words spoken by that student inspired the writing of this book.

I suspect that not a few of us Catholic adults, who have been receiving Holy Communion devoutly for many years, may at one time or another have had thoughts similar to the one expressed by my high school student. I also suspect that many people who do accept fully and believe wholeheartedly in the Real Presence of Jesus in the Eucharist nevertheless have erroneous ideas about the Blessed Sacrament.

The *Catechism of the Catholic Church* (published first in 1992 and revised in 1997) expresses the teaching of the Catholic Church about the Real Presence of Jesus in the Eucharist (#1374) simply, clearly, solemnly, and officially in words originally used by the Council of Trent, in 1551, in its *Decree on the Most Holy Eucharist*. The *Catechism* reads: **"In the most blessed sacrament of the Eucharist 'the body and blood, together with the soul and divinity, of our Lord Jesus Christ and, therefore, *the whole Christ is truly, really, and substantially contained.'"***

The *Decree on the Most Holy Eucharist* itself further declares: **"If anyone denies that the body and blood, together with the soul and divinity, of our Lord Jesus Christ, and therefore, the whole Christ is truly really, and substantially contained in the sacrament of the most holy Eucharist, but says that Christ is present in the Sacrament only as in a sign or figure, or by his power: let him be anathema."**

In no least way whatsoever should anything written in this book be construed to undermine or question the fullness of the teaching of the Church expressed above, which I believe and confess with my whole being. Yes, on every altar, after the Consecration of the Mass, and in every one of the hundreds of thousands of tabernacles in Catholic Churches and chapels around the world, the same Jesus who more than 2000 years ago walked the roads of the Holy Land is really and truly present.

Moreover, please understand that, in the explanations I will give, I am not trying to explain fully the mystery of the Real Presence of Jesus in the Eucharist. This cannot be done. It is a supernatural mystery. There is no way our limited human intelligence can grasp how God brings this about. This is why, The *Decree on the Most Holy Eucharist,* also says, **"We can hardly find words to express this way of existing; but our reason, guided by faith, can know that it is possible for God, and this we should always believe unhesitatingly."**

It is through God's gift of Faith to us that we are able to believe and to be convinced that what we believe about the Eucharist is true, despite our inability to understand it fully by means of our reasoning. On the other hand, through a proper use of our reasoning we can remove erroneous ideas which interfere with our efforts to believe. So, by reflection we can come to see that "it does make sense," even though "we cannot figure out" how God brings about this most marvelous mystery. Moreover, by such reflection, we can deepen our appreciation of the marvelous gift God has given to us in the Eucharist.

St. Thomas Aquinas, the Dominican monk of the thirteenth century who was one of the most outstanding theologians in the history of the Catholic Church, says of the Eucharist, in the beautiful prayer printed just inside the front cover of this book, "Sight, touch, and taste are each deceived in you, but by hearing only can we safely believe. I believe whatever the Son of God has said. Nothing can be more true than this word of him who is the Truth."

And so, it is my hope that, for the ordinary Catholic, this book will clarify the teaching of the Catholic Church on the Real Presence of Jesus in the Eucharist. Even more, by means of its in-depth reflections on the prayers of the Mass, I hope that it will inspire and help Catholics in their daily lives to experience in an ever more meaningful and more enriching way their belief in the Real Presence, their participation in the celebration of the Mass, and their visits to Jesus in the Blessed Sacrament. Furthermore, should a Catholic who has given up belief in the Real Presence of Jesus in the Eucharist happen to read this book, hopefully it will enable that person to realize the truth of this most marvelous gift of God to his Church and thus to accept once again its blessing in his or her life.

I realize, of course, that there are so many other beautiful things which the Church has taught down through the centuries and teaches today about the history of the Holy Eucharist and its Liturgical expression, which I will not speak of in the pages of this book. Many other books have already been written about these matters.

Finally, I wish to express my deep gratitude to the following persons who read through the original manuscript of this book or listened to parts of it read to them; afterwards they kindly provided me with observations and suggestions which were

INTRODUCTION

This book seeks first to clarify for the ordinary Catholic the teaching of the Catholic Church on the nature of the Real Presence of Jesus in the Eucharist. Afterwards it seeks to bring its readers to a deeper appreciation of the Liturgy and especially of the Prayers used in the celebration of the Mass, during which Jesus becomes present on the altar.

In chapter one, we will consider the teaching of the Catholic Church at great length in order to come to a more clear understanding of what the Church actually teaches about the presence of Jesus in the Eucharist.

In chapter two, which presents a theology of the Eucharist, we will examine what really happens during the celebration of the Mass and the significance of Jesus' Eucharistic presence, especially dwelling upon the fact that Jesus is not only present, but He is present in the continuing act of redeeming us through His death on Calvary.

In chapter three, we will examine both the Words of Consecration through which Jesus becomes present on the altar, and also those parts of the four ordinary Eucharistic Prayers which immediately precede or follow these Words of Consecration. We will see that the wording of these prayers expresses the theology of the Eucharist presented in chapter two.

In chapter four, we will study these four ordinary Eucharistic Prayers more extensively and more in depth, in order to understand the meaning of the words the celebrant is praying to God on behalf of the entire congregation. We will notice that sometimes the meaning of the same word changes as it is repeated in different places in the Eucharistic Prayers. We will focus especially on the words gift, offering, oblation, and sacrifice.

In chapter five, we will examine the Ordinary Prayers of the Mass used throughout its celebration, in order to see how their wording is taken from the Bible itself, sometimes using the same words found in Scripture, sometimes a paraphrase, and always expressing the thoughts of Scripture. The Profession of Faith, which is one of the Ordinary Prayers of the Mass on Sundays and other solemn feast days, will also be studied; not so much for the relationship of its wording to Scripture, but to understand more clearly the deep truths which are expressed in the complex and somewhat abstract structure of its phrasing.

Finally, in chapter six, I will share several thoughts or insights which have come to me over the years with regard to the Eucharist: Jesus' presence in the world; "I am with you always;" the identity of Jesus with the Father; visits before the tabernacle; the death of Jesus.

In reading the Prayers of the Mass, as well as Church documents, or even elsewhere in the text, some readers may find words with which they are not familiar. When this happens, readers are invited to look at Appendix I, which gives an explanation of some of these words. If a word is discussed in Appendix I, it will be marked in the text by an asterisk at least once. Appendix I itself will indicate the more important page (or pages) on which words with an asterisk are found. Readers will also find, as they go along, that I explain and discuss some of these words more fully in the text itself.

Appendix II will reflect on the preparation of children for their First Holy Communion.

Appendix III will provide the complete texts of the four ordinary Eucharistic Prayers, for easy reference.

A special word of explanation is needed regarding the footnotes in this book. You will notice that the footnotes are not found at the bottom of the pages on which their numbers occur; rather, they are gathered together at the end of each chapter.

This arrangement seemed more convenient, for the following reasons. First of all, you will find that many of the footnotes are not simply short text references, but they are also much longer than footnotes usually are. This is because in some cases they supply multiple, informative passages from Scripture or from Church documents for deeper reflection. At other times, they involve in-depth discussions about something which has been treated more briefly in the text itself.

Except for chapter four, which has only one footnote, the reader may find it more convenient not to read the footnotes individually at the time they are indicated in the text, but to read them all together after having read the entire chapter.

The footnotes, then, provide a wealth of added material to further enrich the reader's knowledge and understanding and appreciation of the Church's teaching on the Eucharist and the Liturgy of the Mass in which the Eucharist is celebrated.

The ambo in the Cathedral Basilica of St. Louis in St. Louis, Missouri, courtesy of Wikimedia, https://commons.wikimedia.org/wiki/File:Cathedral_Basilica_of_St._Louis_interior_02.jpg

CHAPTER ONE

THE CHURCH'S TEACHING

The Decree on the Most Holy Eucharist

Between 1990 and 2001, about a dozen polls were taken in the United States to determine what Catholics believed about the Real Presence of Jesus in the Eucharist. The first two polls, in 1992 and 1994, taken by Gallup and CBS/New York Times, seemed to indicate that a very large number of Catholics did not believe that Jesus is really and truly present in the Eucharist. The results of these two polls were disputed, however, on the grounds that—at least for some of those who responded—the questions were asked in such a way that their answers did not truly reflect their actual belief.

On the other hand, polls taken both in 2001 and in 2008, by the Center for Applied Research in the Apostolate (CARA), a national research center that is associated with Georgetown University, seemed to reach the same conclusion as the Gallup and CBS/New York Times polls—particularly regarding Catholics whose Sunday Mass attendance was infrequent.

When all was said and done, however, all the polls taken together seemed to indicate that, at least among those who were regularly practicing Catholics, most still did believe in the Real Presence of Jesus in the Eucharist—although, indeed, there has been some decline of belief in this most marvelous mystery of our Catholic Faith.

A number of articles about the polls that had been taken and the conclusions deriving from them appeared in both religious and secular newspapers during this period. In response to the polls that had been taken up to the year 2001, the Catholic Bishops of the United States issued a document, at their General Meeting in June of 2001, entitled *The Real Presence of Jesus Christ in the Sacrament of the Eucharist: Basic Questions and Answers.*[1]

It seems likely that many people who do believe in and accept fully the Real Presence of Jesus in the Eucharist nevertheless have erroneous ideas about the Eucharist. In addition, there are certain common expressions used with reference to the Mass which can be deceiving. These expressions are quite legitimate in themselves and in many cases are merely a practical way of speaking. However, we must be careful that the use of such expressions does not lead us into taking the Mass for granted or thinking of it in a superficial way. For example, we say, "I am going to Mass"; or we ask a priest, "Are you going to say Mass?" "Are you going to do a Mass?" Or, (particularly offensive) in offering a Mass stipend, some ask a priest, "How much is a Mass?" When we consider the true reality and deep sacredness of the Mass, we realize that the Mass is not *bought*; it is not simply *something* that is *said* or *something* one *goes* to. It is not a *spectacle to see or watch*. Rather, the Mass is a most profound liturgical *celebration*. The Mass is the continuing, eternal self-offering of Jesus to His Father in the sacrifice of His death on Calvary. And we *join ourselves* with that self-offering of Jesus by our presence and our participation in the celebration of the Mass.

The false and erroneous misunderstandings which children sometimes get from the way they are taught about the Eucharist are also a problem. I suspect that it is precisely this kind of misunderstanding—if not corrected later in life—which leads some people to a loss of belief in the Real Presence of Jesus in the Eucharist. They think they have to believe something ridiculous which, in fact, the Church does not teach. And so, sadly, they lose the benefit of the exceedingly marvelous Gift which we Catholics have in the Eucharist.

In an effort to correct such erroneous thinking, and to enable ourselves to deepen our appreciation of this "Most Blessed Sacrament" of the Church, let us begin by taking a close look at the Church's teaching as it is expressed so clearly in the *Decree on the Most Holy Eucharist*, from which I quoted briefly in the Preface of this book.

Before we look at the Decree itself however, let us consider the fact that from the very time of the apostles onwards up through the centuries, Catholics have always firmly expressed and repeated their belief in the Real Presence of Jesus in the Eucharist. Moreover, the constant teaching of the Church regarding the Real Presence of Jesus in the Eucharist has been consistent throughout the Church's history and is carried on in our own time in the documents of the Second Vatican Council in 1963 and its aftermath, in *The Catechism of the Catholic Church* in 1997, as well as in other documents of recent Popes. However, what appears to be the clearest expression of the Church's theological teaching about the Eucharist took place when the Council of Trent, under Pope Julius III, issued its *Decree on the Most Holy Eucharist*, on October 11, 1551, at the time of the Protestant Reformation. Even today, the explanation of the Sacrament of the Eucharist which is given in *The Catechism of the Catholic Church* repeatedly refers to this *Decree* of Trent. And so, an examination of this *Decree* seems the most helpful way for us to understand the teaching of the Church about the presence of Jesus in the Eucharist.

Let us take a look, then, at the following partial text of Chapter One of the Decree, along with the text of the Decree's first Canon.[2]

To begin with, the holy council teaches and openly and straightforwardly professes that in the blessed sacrament of the Holy Eucharist, after the consecration of the bread and wine, our Lord Jesus Christ, true God and man, is truly, really, and substantially contained under the perceptible *species* of bread and wine. It is not contradictory to say that our Savior always sits at the right hand of the Father in heaven according to his natural way of existing and that, nevertheless, in his substance* he is sacramentally present in many other places with us. We can hardly find words to express this way of existing; but our reason, guided by faith, can know that it is possible for God, and this we should always believe unhesitatingly. For all our predecessors in the true Church of Christ who treated of this most holy sacrament very clearly professed that our Redeemer instituted this wonderful sacrament at the Last Supper, when, after he had blessed bread and wine, he said in plain, unmistakable words that he was giving them his own body and his own blood. These words are recorded by the Evangelists and afterwards repeated by St. Paul (see Matt. 26:26ff.; Mark 14:22ff.; Luke 22:19ff.; 1Cor.11:23ff.). These words have their proper and obvious meaning and were so understood by the Fathers.

Canon 1. If anyone denies that the body and blood, together with the soul and divinity, of our Lord Jesus Christ, and therefore, the whole Christ is truly, really, and substantially contained in the sacrament of the most holy Eucharist, but says that Christ is present in the Sacrament only as in a sign or figure, or by his power: let him be anathema.*

There are five key words in this document which expresses the Church's teaching about the Real Presence of Jesus in the

Eucharist: <u>truly</u>, <u>really</u>, <u>substantially</u>, <u>substance</u>, and <u>natural</u>. Let's study each of these words.

We begin with the word <u>natural</u>. Immediately after the first sentence, which declares the true and real presence of Jesus in the Eucharist, the Decree continues its teaching by making a distinction between the "natural way of existing" of Jesus and his "sacramental presence" in the Eucharist: *"It is not contradictory to say that our Savior always sits at the right hand of the Father in heaven according to his <u>natural way of existing</u> and that, nevertheless, in his substance he is <u>sacramentally present</u> in many other places with us. We can hardly find words to express this way of existing; but our reason, guided by faith, can know that it is possible for God, and this we should always believe unhesitatingly."*

This distinction made in the Church's teaching between the natural way of existing for Jesus and his way of being truly and really present in the Eucharist, is extremely important. Notice, too, that the Decree is quick to point out two things: first that, "We can hardly find words to express this way of existing," and secondly that, "our reason, guided by faith, can know that it is possible for God"; and so, the Decree concludes, "and this we should always believe unhesitatingly."

A fundamental reality which we must always keep in mind as we study the Eucharist is that there is only one Jesus Christ. We must conclude, then, that although Jesus is not present in the Eucharist in his <u>natural</u> way of existing, still, his Eucharistic presence does not constitute the existence of another distinct being, a separate or new Jesus. Think about it. At the Last Supper, when Jesus, in his natural way of existing, took bread and wine and said, "This is my body," and, "This is my blood," was there one Jesus sitting there saying these words and another Jesus that He was holding in his hand? Of course not!— because there is only one Jesus. This is why the Decree points out that, *"It is not contradictory to say that our Savior always*

9

sits at the right hand of the Father in heaven according to his natural way of existing, and that, nevertheless, in his substance he is sacramentally present in many other places with us. We can hardly find words to express this way of existing...."

Notice then, that on the one hand, in the passage quoted above, the Church clearly teaches that the real Presence of Jesus in the Eucharist is not his <u>natural way of existing</u>. On the other hand, when the Decree says, *"We can hardly find words to express this way of existing,"* it explicitly teaches that the Presence of Jesus in the Eucharist is a <u>way of existing</u>. As I have said, it is not a new or separate existence of Jesus, but rather another *way*, another *manner*, another *mode* of existing—distinct from his natural way of existing—in which the one Jesus makes himself present. Furthermore, precisely because it is not the natural way in which Jesus exists, but a different way of being present, there is no question of "squeezing a man into a tiny host." My student's problem arose from the fact that he thought Jesus is present in the Eucharist in his natural way of existing.

Now consider the words <u>truly</u> and <u>really</u>. It is fairly easy for us to understand what the Church means when it says that Jesus is *truly* and *really* present in the Eucharist. <u>Truly</u> is the adverb form of the adjective <u>true</u>. When we use the word <u>true</u>, we are speaking not about a thing in itself, but about our knowledge of the thing. Things are what they are. If our knowledge of something is accurate and correct, we say it is <u>true</u>. If our knowledge is mistaken, we say it is false or not true. For example, if it is raining heavily outside, but we say that it is a clear day, our statement is not true; it is false, because it does not correspond to the reality.

Again, <u>really</u> is the adverb form of the adjective <u>real</u>. When we say something is <u>real</u>, we mean that it is not imaginary; it is not phony or false; it is not artificial; it is not an imitation; it is not a sign or symbol or copy of something, or a picture of it; but it is actual; it is the thing itself, actually here and now physically existing before us. And so, when the Church says that Jesus is truly and really present in the Eucharist, it is using the words truly and really in the sense in which we ordinarily understand them. Jesus is actually there, and so it is true to say that He is there. Yes, the teaching of the Church is that Jesus is truly and really present in the Eucharist.

Finally, consider the word substance* (along with its adverb form, substantially, which the *Decree on the Most Holy Eucharist* uses in its first Canon). Let's take a closer look again at what the Church teaches in Chapter One of the Decree.

After stating that *"our Savior always sits at the right hand of the Father in heaven according to his natural way of existing,"* the *Decree* continues, *"...nevertheless, in his sub-stance he is sacramentally present in many other places with us."*

What does the Church's teaching mean when it says that Jesus is sacramentally present *in his substance*? The word substance (including the adverb form) is a technical word used in the study of philosophy. In talking about the presence of Jesus in the Eucharist, the Church is saying something much more specific and technical than what we mean when we ordinarily use the word substance (and its other forms) in everyday speech with its various meanings. For example, we say that honey is a thick substance compared to water, or that there is no substance to someone's opinion or that the evidence of a crime is pretty substantial, or that a news report is substantially accurate, etc.

What, then, is the special technical philosophical meaning of the word substance as used in the Church's teaching about the Real Presence of Jesus in the Eucharist?

Because of its complexity, I won't try at this point to give a precise, accurate explanation using philosophical terminology itself, with its carefully distinguished technical concepts. I'll leave that to a footnote a little later for those who may wish to investigate more deeply the concept of "substance" (along with a discussion of the related philosophical term <u>accident</u>*).[3] Here, instead, let me use a simple non-philosophical example, which I hope will nonetheless provide an accurate understanding of the philosophical meaning of the word <u>substance</u>.

I like to use the example of a car or automobile, although an automobile actually has many parts and is made up of other things, each with its own substance, such as glass, metal, cloth, rubber, plastic, etc.—all the things from which an automobile is made. Still, to talk about "what makes an automobile be an automobile, or what the *substance* of an automobile is," seems like a legitimate, simple, and clear way to help you understand the philosophical meaning of <u>substance</u>. So here it is.

What, then, is an automobile? Well, an automobile is an object which is made up of tires, wheels, brakes, rear-view mirrors, a motor, transmission gears and a handle to shift them, axles, a gas tank, a muffler and tail pipe, headlights and tail lights, bumpers, windows, doors, seats, a steering wheel, brake and accelerator pedals, a dashboard with dials that indicate various things like speed, the amount of miles travelled, battery power, amount of fuel, etc. Most automobiles today have not only radios, but also CD players; and some even have a voice that tells you when you are running out of gas; and possibly a GPS, which helps you find your way to a particular place, as well as several other parts and features which I haven't mentioned— not to mention new features being constantly invented.

Now, what if I take off the rear-view mirrors; is it still an automobile? What if I take off the front or rear lights; is it still an automobile? What if I take out the windows and even take off the doors; is it still an automobile? What if I remove the bumpers? Is it still an automobile?

Do you see where my questions are leading? We can make a

lot of changes in an automobile, but it still remains an automobile. And so for a while, we can keep saying, "Yes, it's still an automobile." However, at some point, as we tear it down, it is no longer an automobile. It is arguable as to just what that point is. But there is such a point, and when that point is reached, what was an automobile before, is now no longer an automobile, because it no longer has the *substance* of an automobile. At this point it has lost its *substance*. *Substance*, then, means "that element in the make-up of any being which accounts for its being what it is."

And so, when we are talking about an automobile, the philosophical word <u>substance</u> means "whatever it takes to have an automobile," even if it doesn't have everything an automobile usually has.

Now let us apply this understanding of *substance* to the presence of Jesus in the Eucharist. This is the sense in which the teaching of the Church, as expressed in the *Decree on the Most Holy Eucharist*, uses the words <u>substance</u> and <u>substantially</u>: everything it takes to actually have Jesus really and truly present is there in the consecrated host and wine—but not everything about Jesus.

For example, the distinction itself which the Church's teaching makes between Jesus' natural way of existing and his Eucharistic way of existing, implies that in his Eucharistic presence, the characteristics of Jesus' body and blood are not visible as they are in his natural way of existing. That's why we cannot see his hands or his arms, etc. Again, as I've said before, that's also why we don't have to worry about "squeezing a man into a tiny host." Since it is a question of the one Jesus being really, truly, substantially present, but in a way which is not his natural way of existing, how big Jesus is in his natural way of existing or how tiny the sacramental host is in which he is substantially present doesn't make any difference. As long as there is everything it takes to have Jesus (even if it is not everything about Jesus) it is possible to have the whole Jesus really, truly, and substantially present in the Eucharist.

In fact, according to the Church's teaching, after the Consecration of the Mass *the substances of bread or wine* are no longer present. But the *other natural characteristics* of bread and wine do remain after the Consecration, no longer with the *substances* of bread and wine, but now along with the *substance of Jesus.* The *Decree* refers to this reality when it says that Jesus is "*substantially contained under the perceptible species* of bread and wine.*"4

Think of it this way: after the priest prays the words of Consecration over the bread, what really makes bread be bread is not there any longer. And so, even though it still looks and tastes and feels like bread, it is not bread anymore. On the other hand, what made it really be bread, that is, its *substance*, has now been changed into the *substance* of Jesus, that is, changed into what makes Jesus really be Jesus. And so Jesus, not bread, is now really "in the host," really present in what, in its outward appearances, still looks and feels and tastes like bread. But the appearances of bread no longer "have what it takes" to be bread; they are no longer supported by the *substance* of bread; they are now supported by God's miraculous power along with the *substance* of Jesus. And although there is no way we can actually see or experience any change in the host after the words of Consecration, the reality is, in fact, that the host has changed from having both the *substance* and the appearances of bread now to having the *substance* of Jesus, while still keeping only the appearances of bread. (What we have said here applies also to the wine after the priest prays over it the words of Consecration.)

As *The Catechism of the Catholic Church* points out (#1376), in Chapter 4 and in Canon 2 of the *Decree on the Most Holy Eucharist*, the Church's teaching further explains that this change of the *substances* of bread and wine into the *substance* of Jesus—without changing the other characteristics of bread and wine—is fittingly and properly to be called by the name *transubstantiation*. This word literally means "the crossing over of a substance." That is, the *substance of Jesus* has "crossed over" into the other characteristics of bread and wine (which the *Decree* refers to as the "species" of bread and wine) and replaced the *substances* of bread and of wine; so that now, what still looks and feels and tastes like bread and wine is actually the *substance* of Jesus, not the *substances* of bread or wine. *Transubstantiation* has taken place.

And so the one risen Jesus, who, *in his natural way of existing*, continues to exist both *in substance and with all his other natural characteristics*, at the right hand of the Father in heaven, has, at the same time, through the miraculous power of God, now really and truly become also substantially present on the altar in the species of bread and wine.

We must not—because we cannot—try to imagine how Jesus is present in the consecrated host (or consecrated wine). It is absolutely impossible for human reason to figure this out. Our reason does indeed help us to realize that God certainly has the miraculous power to make Jesus present in the consecrated appearances of bread and wine; and so we can see that "it does make sense." But our reason cannot understand <u>how</u> God brings this about. This is why the Church tells us, *"We can hardly find words to express this way of existing, but our reason, guided by Faith, can know that it is possible for God, and this we should always believe unhesitatingly."*

Let us sum up, then, what the Catholic Church teaches about the Eucharist. When the priest celebrating Mass prays the words of Consecration over the bread and wine, their substances are totally changed into the substance of Jesus. And while it is not his natural way of existing in heaven with God, still, absolutely everything needed to have this same Jesus is now really, truly and substantially contained in the mere species, or appearances, of bread and wine which remain on the altar.

And so what was, moments before, merely a piece of bread and some wine now only looks and tastes and feels like bread and wine. But having lost what it takes actually to be bread and wine, it now contains instead everything that it takes to have and actually to be Jesus. And so the whole Christ—body and blood, soul and divinity—is now really and truly present under the appearances of bread and wine. The same identical Jesus who walked the roads of the Holy Land two thousand years ago—even if not in the same natural way of existing but in a mysterious, miraculous, and extraordinary way of existing—is really and truly present with us now in the Eucharist.

If we stop to think about it, there are a number of situations in our lives in which you and I know and are certain of the presence of something, even though we cannot see or hear or touch it at the time; for example, the existence of the sun when it is night time, or the existence of radio waves, which we don't feel or see but which cause the sound when we turn on a radio. Another example would be the experience of being in a pitch dark cave with others. If everyone stands absolutely still and makes no sound and if we stand far enough away from one another so that we cannot reach out to touch anyone; then, even though we have no experience of the others in the cave with us, we know for sure that they are there.

Our experience of the presence of Jesus in the Eucharist is something like this. We know he's really and truly there; but because it is not in his natural way of existing we can't see or hear or touch him. Therefore, as I have said, we shouldn't strain our minds to try to imagine his presence. On the other hand, we should definitely and fully accept the fact that he is there; and we should try to realize what an exceedingly marvelous reality is this real and true presence of Jesus with us. Think of it! Each time a Mass is offered, the same Jesus who walked and talked on earth two thousand years ago really and truly becomes present on the altar. And in every place that the Blessed Sacrament is kept in a tabernacle, that same Jesus is really and truly there. **The most important thing in this whole discussion is for us to realize that in the Eucharist Jesus Himself is actually here with us—just as he told us, "I am with you always!" (Mt. 28, 20)**

Again recall the Church's teaching, "*We can hardly find words to express this way of existing; but our reason, guided by faith, can know that it is possible for God, and this we should always believe unhesitatingly.*" What a magnificent and most marvelous gift our God has given us in the Real Presence of Jesus in the Eucharist!

There is something else said in the *Decree on the Most Holy Eucharist* which we must examine more carefully. In speaking of the New Testament accounts of the institution of the Eucharist by Jesus at the Last supper, the Decree makes references to the Gospels of St. Matthew, St. Mark, St. Luke, and also to St. Paul's First Letter to the Corinthians. Notice that no reference is given to St. John's Gospel (see page 8). John is the only one of the four evangelists who does not give an account of the institution of the Eucharist. However, what St. John does say about the Last Supper is very important in relationship to the institution of the Eucharist. St John tells us that at the Last Supper (before He instituted the Eucharist) Jesus washed the feet of the disciples and told them that they must imitate him in serving others. Our experience of the Eucharist, then, and what Jesus meant it to be for us must include this command for us to serve others. The Eucharist is not just a matter of our personal union with Jesus in Holy Communion. It also obliges and enables us to imitate Jesus in serving others. If we accept our very special relationship with Jesus in the Eucharist, we must also accept his teaching about the service of others.

Moreover, even though St. John's Gospel does not mention

the actual institution of the Eucharist, it does teach, even more forcefully than any of the other Scriptural references, the truth of the Real Presence of Jesus in the Eucharist. Christians had been living out and celebrating their wholehearted belief in the Real Presence of Jesus in the Eucharist for decades before St. John even wrote his Gospel. And so, in the light of this belief John records, in chapter six of his Gospel, the insistence of Jesus, despite the objections of some of his listeners, that he truly gives people his body as food and his blood as drink. The more his listeners objected, the more Jesus insisted. And when many of them stopped following him, walked away, and said that what he was saying was too hard to believe, Jesus did not back down. Rather, he turned to his twelve apostles and asked them, "Are you going away, too?" Peter replied so wonderfully, "Lord, to whom shall we go? You have the words of eternal life; and we believe and have come to know that you are the Holy One of God."

So then, although St. John's Gospel does not explicitly give an account of the institution of the Eucharist, what it has to say about the Real Presence of Jesus in the Eucharist is very important in our understanding of the Eucharist.[5]

One final thought. At the Last Supper, when He instituted the Eucharist, Jesus was simultaneously present both in his natural way of existing and in his new Eucharistic way of existing. The next day on Calvary, Jesus was present on the cross only in his natural way of existing. Today, in the celebration of the Mass, Jesus is present, not in his natural way of existing, but really, truly, and substantially in his Eucharistic, sacramental, way of being present. But it is the same Jesus, really and truly present, whether in his natural way of existing or his special Eucharistic way of existing. The apostles, then, knew and experienced this one Jesus in three different ways: in his natural way of existing before his death; in his natural way of existing after his resurrection; and in his Eucharistic way of existing. While we are on earth, we know the same Jesus the apostles knew and experienced; but we encounter him only in his Eucharistic way of existing or we pray to him, unseen, in Heaven. After death, we too will personally encounter him in his natural risen way of existing. But it will be the same Jesus we have known all our lives in the Eucharist.

I repeat what I said earlier. What a magnificent and most marvelous gift our God has given us in the Real Presence of Jesus in the Eucharist!

Endnotes for Chapter 1

[1] To order *The Real Presence of Jesus Christ in the Sacrament of the Eucharist: Basic Questions and Answers* in its official published format, contact USCCB Publishing Services, 800-235-8722. Pub. No. 5-434.

[2] The Council of Trent published its teachings on various beliefs and practices of the Catholic Church, first by way of a long prose text explaining a particular doctrine. These prose texts were called **"Decrees"** and were divided into **"Chapters."** After each Decree there was added a numbered series of short, specific statements, often in negative form, referring to a person's denial of Church teaching (e.g. "if anyone denies," etc.). These statements were called **"Canons"** and were intended to reject specific errors and to clarify without question what a Catholic must believe about a given doctrine in order to remain in good standing in the Catholic Church. Each canon concluded with the official formula, **"let him be anathema,"** which meant, let such a disbeliever be excommunicated from the Catholic Church.

In this book texts of the Council of Trent are quoted from the English translation found in *The Church Teaches*, B. Herder Book Co. 15&17 South Broadway, St. Louis 2, Mo. 1955 (Fifth Printing, 1962) Library of Congress Catalog Card Number: 55-10397.

[3] A WORD OF CAUTION: *What is said below in footnote 3 has*

been simplified from what would be found in an actual textbook of philosophy. Nevertheless, it contains subject matter which the reader may find difficult to follow, especially if he or she has never studied philosophy in college. I suggest, then, to you, the reader, that you do not try to read this footnote until after you have first read completely through the entire text of chapter one. Then, if you are interested, come back at a later time and work your way through the explanation given here in footnote 3.

Without trying to give an exhaustive explanation of the concepts "substance" and "accident," such as would be found in a philosophy textbook, still, for those who might be interested, I would like to add the following explanation that is philosophically more exact than the "automobile" explanation given in the text.

When we observe objects around us, including ourselves, we notice that they change and yet they remain the same. Changes in living things are the easiest to observe. For example, a growing flower-plant changes constantly from its seed-generated root to developing a stem, then leaves, buds, and flowers which vary in size and number. But it always remains the same plant, despite its constant changes.

Next, we must consider a fundamental truth in the study of philosophy which is known as the "Principle of Contradiction." This Principle states: a thing cannot both be and not be at the same time and in the same respect. That is, something cannot exist and not exist simultaneously. For example, a plant cannot be both living and not living at the same time. True, a plant can be living in some of its parts and dead in others; one leaf can be dead, another alive. But the same leaf or same particular part of a leaf cannot be both alive and dead at the same time. It is either one or the other. It is either alive or not alive, that is, dead. So, too, when the entire plant dies, it is in no way alive, but only dead.

The truth expressed by this Principle of Contradiction is obvious; it is self-evident and does not need to be proved by further arguments. Now let us apply this principle of contradiction to the phenomenon of changing things.

The reality in a being by reason of which it is what it is and always remains the same being, even though it undergoes changes, cannot simultaneously be the same reality in that being by reason of which it undergoes the changes. This would require that "to-remain-the-same" and "to-change" be identical. Clearly they are not. They are the exact opposite to each other. They are "contradictory" to each other. Therefore, a being which both remains the same yet changes must be somehow "composite." It must be "made up of" or have within itself two different elements or "principles" of its being, one which enables it to change and the other which enables it simultaneously to remain the same being that it is. These principles do not exist as separate beings, but only as distinct components of the existing being in which they are found.

The name which philosophers give to the principle which accounts for something being what it is and always remaining the same in its being is *substance* (from the Latin *sub stans*, meaning "standing under"). The principle which accounts for changes in the being which remains the same is called *accident* (from the Latin *ac cidens*, meaning "happening to"). So then, we must say that any given created thing that exists is made up of substance and accident. Moreover, while the substance of any given being is invisible to our senses and can only be known intellectually, the changeable components of a being, that is, its accidents—such as size, shape, weight, color, texture, temperature, etc.—are visible to our senses; and so we easily observe the "accidental" changes which take place in beings which remain "substantially" the same.

And so changes which take place in any being while it continues to be the same being are called "accidental" changes. But there can also be a "substantial" change. This would be a final change which causes the being in question to cease from being what it is and become something else. For example, when a living being dies it undergoes a "substantial" change. It no longer has the same substance it had before death, and so it is not the same kind of being it was before the change. We know this because living things and dead things act in completely different ways; and the substance of what a thing is becomes known by reason of what it does, because of its actions. For example, living things move and grow, while dead things cease such activity and gradually decompose into various lifeless elements. And so, because a living thing and a dead thing act in totally different ways, when a living being becomes a dead being, we know that it has undergone a change in its substance, a substantial change.

Hopefully this rather tedious philosophical reflection on the meaning of *substance* and *accident* will help you towards a deeper understanding of what the Church teaches when it uses the words substance and substantially in speaking of Christ's Real Presence in the Eucharist.

4 The *Decree on the Most Holy Eucharist* uses the word "species" (of bread and wine), which in this case is simply a synonym for the more philosophical word "accidents" (of bread and wine). And since the accidents of a being can be perceived through our senses, the "species" are said to be "perceptible." The relationship between substance and accidents is explained above in footnote 3.

5 References to the Eucharist are found in the following passages of the New Testament.

As happens commonly in the Synoptic Gospels, there are variations in the accounts.

Matt. 26, 26-29

During the meal Jesus took bread, blessed it, broke it, and gave it to his disciples. "Take this and eat it," he said, "this is my body." Then he took the cup, gave thanks, and gave it to them. "All of you must drink from it," he said, "for this is my blood, the blood of the covenant, to be poured out in behalf of many for the forgiveness of sins. I tell you, I will not drink this fruit of the vine from now until the day when I drink it new with you in my Father's reign."

Mark 14, 22-25

During the meal he took bread, blessed and broke it, and gave it to them. "Take this," he said, "this is my body." He likewise took a cup, gave thanks and passed it to them, and they all drank from it. He said to them, "This is my blood, the blood of the covenant, to be poured out on behalf of many. I solemnly assure you, I will never again drink of the fruit of the vine until the day when I drink it new in the reign of

God."

Luke 22, 19-20

Then, taking bread and giving thanks, he broke it and gave it to them, saying: "This is my body to be given for you. Do this as a remembrance of me." He did the same with the cup after eating, saying as he did so: "This cup is the new covenant in my blood, which will be shed for you."

1 Cor. 10, 16-17

Is not the cup of blessing we bless a sharing in the blood of Christ? And is not the bread we break a sharing in the body of Christ? Because the loaf of bread is one, we, many though we are, are one body, for we all partake of the one loaf."

1 Cor. 11, 23-29

I received from the Lord what I handed on to you, namely that the Lord Jesus on the night in which he was betrayed took bread, and after he had given thanks, broke it and said, "This is my body, which is for you. Do this in remembrance of me." In the same way, after the supper, he took the cup, saying, "This cup is the new covenant in my blood. Do this whenever you drink it, in remembrance of me." Every time, then, you eat this bread and drink this cup, you proclaim the death of the Lord until he comes! This means that whoever eats the bread or drinks the cup of the Lord unworthily sins against the body and blood of the Lord. A man should examine himself first; only then should he eat of the bread and drink of the cup. He who eats and drinks without recognizing the body eats and drinks a judgment on himself.

John 6, 32-69

Jesus said to them: "I solemnly assure you, it was not Moses who gave you bread from the heavens; it is my Father who gives you the real heavenly bread. God's bread comes down from heaven and gives life to the world." "Sir, give us this bread always," they besought him. Jesus explained to them: "I myself am the bread of life. No one who comes to me shall ever be hungry, and no one who believes in me shall ever thirst. But as I told you—though you have seen me, you still do not believe. All that the Father gives me shall come to me; no one who comes will I ever reject, because it is not to do my own will that I have come down from heaven, but to do the will of him who sent me. It is the will of him who sent me that I should lose nothing of what he has given me; rather, that I should raise it up on the last day. Indeed, this is the will of my Father, that everyone who looks upon the Son and believes in him shall have eternal life. Him I will raise up on the last day."

At this the Jews started to murmur in protest because he claimed, "I am the bread that came down from heaven." They kept saying: "Is this not Jesus, the son of Joseph? Do we not know his father and mother? How can he claim to have come down from heaven?" "Stop your murmuring," Jesus told them. "No one can come to me unless the Father who sent me draws him; I will raise him up on the last day. It is written in the prophets: 'They shall all be taught by God.' Everyone who has heard the Father and learned from Him comes to me. Not that anyone has seen the Father —only the one who is from God has seen the Father. Let me firmly assure you, he who believes has eternal life. I am the bread of life. Your ancestors ate manna in the desert, but they died. This is the bread that comes down from heaven for a man to eat and never die. I myself am the living bread come down from heaven. If anyone eats this bread he shall live forever; the bread I will give is my flesh, for the life of the world." At this the Jews quarreled among themselves saying, "How can he give us his flesh to eat?" Thereupon Jesus said to them: "Let me solemnly assure you, if you do not eat the flesh of the Son of Man and drink his blood, you have no life in you. He who feeds on my flesh and drinks my blood has life eternal, and I will raise him up on the last day. For my flesh is real food and my blood real drink. The man who feeds on my flesh and drinks my blood remains in me, and I in him. Just as the Father who has life sent me and I have life because of the Father, so the man who feeds on me will have life because of me. This is the bread that came down from heaven. Unlike your ancestors who ate and died nonetheless, the man who feeds on this bread shall live forever." He said this in a synagogue instruction at Capernaum.

After hearing these words, many of his disciples remarked, "This sort of talk is hard to endure! How can anyone take it seriously?" Jesus was fully aware that his disciples were murmuring in protest at what he had said. "Does it shake your faith?" he asked them. "What, then, if you were to see the Son of Man ascend to where he was before...? It is the spirit that gives life; the flesh is useless. The words I spoke to you are spirit and life. Yet among you there are some who do not believe." (Jesus knew from the start, of course, the ones who refused to believe, and the one who would hand him over.) He went on to say: "This is why I have told you that no one can come to me unless it is granted him by the Father."

From this time on, many of his disciples broke away and would not remain in his company any longer. Jesus then said to the Twelve, "Do you want to leave me too?" Simon Peter answered him, "Lord to whom shall we go? You have the words of eternal life. We have come to believe; we are convinced that you are God's holy one."

Holy Family Catholic Church (North Baltimore, Ohio) - stained glass, Eucharist, courtesy of Wikimedia, https://commons.wikimedia.org/wiki/File:Holy_Family_Catholic_Church_(North_Baltimore,_Ohio)_-_stained_glass,_Eucharist.jpg

CHAPTER TWO

THE MASS EXPLAINED

A Theology of the Eucharist

Some readers may have found my explanation of the Real Presence of Jesus in the Eucharist a bit "heavy." But this was necessary due to the inherently philosophical nature of those reflections. Hopefully this chapter will read more easily. Nevertheless, it is not enough for us simply to understand more clearly the <u>fact</u> of Jesus' Real Presence in itself. We must now reflect further on the manner in which Jesus becomes present, why he becomes present, and our response to his presence on the altar as we assist in the celebration of the Mass.

It is during the celebration of the Mass that Jesus Christ, through the priest's words of Consecration, becomes truly, really, and substantially present on the altar. This, of course, is precisely what makes the Mass uniquely important and different from all other ways of praying—whether we pray individually or in community with other people.

After his life, death, and resurrection in his natural way of existing on earth, Jesus ascended into heaven, so that now his only natural way of existing is in his risen life. And so it is in this risen life in heaven (still with all the memories of his former life on earth, of course) that he constantly remains "at the right hand of the Father, in his <u>natural way of existing</u>. But, as we have seen, this one and the same risen Jesus, by a miracle of God's power, simultaneously becomes truly, really, and <u>substantially present sacramentally</u> in the Eucharist under the appearances of bread and wine, in many places around the world.

And so, I invite you to ask yourself the question, "Why does Jesus become present on the altar during the Mass?" To find the answer this question, we must reflect on two different aspects of the death of Jesus: its uniqueness as a saving act, and what it was about his death that made it redemptive.

First let us look at several passages from the **Letter to the Hebrews** in the New Testament.[1]

In **chapter 7, verses 26 to 28**, we read, "It was fitting that we should have such a high priest: holy, innocent, undefiled, separated from sinners, higher than the heavens. Unlike the other high priests, *he has no need to offer sacrifice day after day*, first for his own sins[2] and then for those of the People; *he did that once for all* when he offered himself. For the law sets up as high priests men who are weak, but the word of the oath which came after the law appoints as priest the Son made perfect forever."

In **chapter 9, verses 24 to 28**, we read, "For Christ did not enter into a sanctuary made by hands, a mere copy of the true one; he entered into heaven itself that he might appear before God now on our behalf. *Not that he might offer himself there again and again*, as the high priest enters year after year into the sanctuary with blood that is not his own; if that were so, he would have had to suffer death over and over from the creation of the world. But now he has appeared at the end of the ages to take away sins *once for all* by his sacrifice. Just as it is appointed that men die once, and after death be judged, so *Christ was offered up once* to take away the sins of many."

Again, in **chapter 10, verses 12 to 14**, we read, "But Jesus *offered one sacrifice for sins* and took his seat forever at the right hand of God; now he waits until his enemies are placed beneath his feet. By *one offering* he has forever perfected those who are being sanctified."

In the above passages the Letter to the Hebrews tells us repeatedly (see the italics) that Jesus has redeemed us once and for all by his death on Calvary.

Now, since Jesus Christ offered Himself up in sacrifice for the human race once and for all on Calvary, and since Jesus now sits forever at the right hand of the Father interceding for us in his natural, risen way of existing; he does not need to be sacramentally present on the altar in order to offer himself up again for us. There is nothing more he himself needs to do to achieve our redemption. Moreover, there is nothing—so to speak –that he could do on the altar sacramentally that he could not do just as well or better where he is already "face to face" with God his Father.

To help us further in understanding the purpose of the real presence of Jesus on the altar in the Mass, let us next reflect on the nature of the redeeming death of Jesus on Calvary. Remember, when Jesus instituted the Eucharist at the Last Supper, he related it to the death he would die the next day. He said, "This is my body which is given for you," and "This is my blood of the covenant which is poured out for many."

This leads to another question, which can be asked in various ways: how did Jesus redeem us by dying on a cross? Or, why is it that the death of Jesus redeemed us?

For our answer to this latter question we turn first to St. Paul, then to St. Thomas Aquinas, and afterwards once again to the Letter to the Hebrews.

In his **Letter to the Philippians, chapter 2, verses 5 to 11**, St. Paul writes:

"Your attitude must be that of Christ: Though he was in the

form of God He did not deem equality with God something to be grasped at. Rather, he emptied himself and took the form of a slave, being born in the likeness of men. He was known to be of human estate, and it was thus that he humbled himself, *obediently accepting even death, death on a cross!* Because of this God highly exalted him and bestowed on him the name above every other name, so that at Jesus' name every knee must bend in heaven, on earth, and under the earth, and every tongue proclaim to the glory of God the Father: Jesus Christ is Lord!"

Here is what St. Thomas says in his famous work, the Summa Theologica, part III, question 48, article 2:

"*I answer that* He properly atones for an offense who offers something which the offended one loves equally, or even more than he detested the offense. But by suffering out of love and obedience, Christ gave more to God than was required to compensate for the offense of the whole human race. First of all, because of the exceeding charity from which he suffered; secondly, on account of the dignity of His life which He laid down in atonement, for it was the life of One who was God and man; thirdly, on account of the extent of the Passion, and the greatness of the grief endured ... ."[3]

Look also, again, at the **Letter to the Hebrews, chapter 10, verses 5 to 10**:

"Wherefore, on coming into the world, Jesus said: "Sacrifice and offering you did not desire, but a body you have prepared for me; Holocausts and sin offerings you took no delight in. Then I said, 'As is written of me in the book, I have come to do your will, O God.' " First he says, "Sacrifices and offerings, holocausts and sin offerings, you neither desired nor delighted in." (These are offered according to the prescriptions* of the law.) Then he says, "I have come to do your will." In other words, he takes away the first covenant to establish the second. By this "will" we have been sanctified through the offering of the body of Jesus Christ once for all."

What do these three texts tell us about how the death of Jesus on Calvary brought about our redemption?

First, St. Paul speaks of the <u>obedience</u> of Jesus, even to death on the cross. Then St. Thomas says that Jesus redeemed us by suffering out of <u>love and obedience</u> and that, while the dignity of Jesus' life as the God-man and the terrible suffering of his passion and death were truly active factors in our redemption, the primary cause in that redemption was the <u>exceeding love</u> with which Jesus died on the cross. Finally, in the Letter to the Hebrews, both the words of Jesus—"I have come to do your will, O God"—and the words—"By this 'will' we have been sanctified through the offering of the body of Jesus Christ once for all"— seem to confirm the teachings of St. Paul and St. Thomas. For, God's will to save us is realized through the will of Jesus to accept and to do God's will, even to death.

Now, Jesus Christ never changes these sentiments of total love and obedience, his will, even to death, to do his Father's will. He keeps them for all eternity at the right hand of His Father in Heaven. Since in his natural way of existing, He offered himself once and for all, when he was crucified to death on Calvary; and since there is only one Jesus Christ, when He becomes present on the altar in his Eucharistic way of existing, it is with these same eternal redeeming sentiments, the identical ones he had as he hung on the cross on Calvary. And since, as we have seen, it is these sentiments in his act of dying which bring about our redemption, we can say that on the altar, as far as the most important feature of his death is concerned, that is, in what actually made his death redemptive, Jesus is with us in his very act of redeeming us. The miracle of the Eucharist is that, after the words of Consecration during the Mass, time and space fall away, so to speak, and—two thousand years later—we are present with Christ in his redeeming act itself. Properly understood, we can truly say that after the Consecration, we are *At Mass with Jesus on Calvary!*

Surely this is what is meant when the Church teaches, in Papal encyclicals and in various other documents, that the Holy Sacrifice of the Mass is the same sacrifice as Calvary, but in an un-bloody manner. Can we not say truly—understood proper-ly—not only that the Sacrifice of the Mass is the same sacrifice <u>as</u> Calvary, but that the Sacrifice of the Mass <u>is</u> Calvary, made present in our own time? At Mass, the same, identical Jesus is present with the same sentiments which brought about our redemption on Calvary. Through the miracle of the Eucharist and God's overwhelming love and almighty power, Jesus is present with all Catholics, down through the centuries, in the actual, continuing moment of his total self-offering in love and obedience which brings about our redemption.[4]

I repeat once more: What a magnificent and most marvelous gift our God has given us in the Real Presence of Jesus in the Eucharist! I urge you to read the beautiful passages from a few of the Church documents themselves.[5]

Now we can answer our original question, "Why does Jesus become present on the altar?"

Jesus becomes present on the altar in order to bring Calvary to us. Since "by one offering he has forever perfected those who are being sanctified" (Heb. 10:14), Jesus does not become present on the altar to bring about our redemption. He has already done this. Therefore, it is not for his own sake, but for our sake that he becomes present on the altar. By his Real

Presence in the Mass, Jesus brings Calvary to us, and thus offers us the supreme opportunity to join ourselves with him in his eternal act of total surrender to God. And since the presence of Jesus on the altar adds nothing new to his redeeming action in itself, except to become actually and immediately present with us in this redeeming action, it is I myself who must bring something <u>new</u> to each Mass regarding my redemption. From a certain point of view and speaking practically, the Mass will be of little or no value for me, except to the extent that I truly offer myself and my daily living to God the Father in union with Christ. Therefore, as far as I am able I should try, along with him, to have the same sentiments he has of total self-surrender to God in love and obedience. Yes, if the sentiments of Jesus are so important in bringing about our redemption, so are our sentiments in accepting our redemption. In every Mass we should offer ourselves to God in union with Jesus, in as full a gift of ourselves as we are able to make at the time. Our desire to make such an offering should be the reason why we participate in the celebration of Mass.

The above thoughts, by the way, provide the best response to people who say "I don't like to go to Mass, because I don't get anything out of it." How much a person "gets out of the Mass" is going to depend upon "how much he or she "puts into the Mass."

This, then, is what the Mass is all about. It is Christ's way of bringing each generation of Catholics, down through the centuries, into immediate union with himself, so that they can join with him as he offers himself in perfect love and obedience to God the Father to save us from our sins and bring us to eternal life. This is why Jesus becomes present on the altar!

Finally, let us reflect on the nature of "sacrifice." We speak of the Mass as the Holy Sacrifice of the Mass. What is a "sacrifice" in the religious sense of this word? A "sacrifice" is a religious ceremony during which some kind of offering, often an animal, is made to a god. Some peoples in history have even offered human sacrifices to their gods. In the Hebrew tradition of God's Chosen People their offering to the one true God was often a lamb. The offering, also called the victim, was slaughtered and burned up in the sacrifice, although sometimes parts of the animal being offered were only cooked and then saved to be eaten afterwards by those on behalf of whom the sacrifice was being offered. Participation in this meal was a sign of the person's involvement in and commitment to the purpose of the sacrifice. Sacrifices were offered for four main reasons: as a sign of adoration of the god to whom the sacrifice was offered; as a sign of thanksgiving to the god for favors received; to make petitions to the god for particular needs; and, finally, as a sign of "satisfaction," that is, to show sorrow for sins committed against the god and to make-up for them by the sacrifice. Of course, the very act of joining with a priest in the offering of a sacrifice brought about and fostered a certain union of those offering the sacrifice, both with the god to whom the sacrifice was offered, and with one another.

Let us apply all this, then, to our participation in the Holy Sacrifice of the Mass. We participate in the celebration of the Mass so that, in union with Jesus—now present on the altar in his eternal Sacrifice—we can offer to God the Father the successes and good qualities of our own lives, in adoration and in thanksgiving. In satisfaction we also offer our failures and sins to God with contrition, in order that He might forgive them and help us to overcome them. And we petition God for the things we need, especially His Grace.

When we actively and consciously and fully participate in the prayers and actions of the Mass, we do make such a sacrificial offering in a very explicit way. In doing so, and especially in receiving Holy Communion, we publicly show that we are keeping the New and Eternal Covenant God has made with us through the death of Christ.[6] We are proclaiming what the death and resurrection of Christ means for human beings.

Finally, by listening together to God's Word in Scripture, by our <u>common</u> act of Worship as a Community, and because we all receive the Body and Blood of the one Christ, all those participating in the celebration of Mass grow in their union with God and are drawn together into greater unity as a Christian Community; and so they are strengthened to exert a stronger Christianizing influence in the world.[7]

Endnotes for Chapter 2

[1] Throughout this book, (unless noted otherwise) Scripture quotations are given from <u>The New American Bible</u>, First Edition, The Catholic Press, Publishers; Distributed by The World Publishing Company; Copyright 1970, by the Confraternity of Christian Doctrine, Washington, D.C.

Quotations from the Catechism of the Catholic Church are given from <u>Catechism of the Catholic Church</u>, Second edition, *revised in accordance with the official Latin text promulgated by Pope Saint John Paul II*. English translation of the Catechism of the Catholic Church: *Modifications from the Editio Typica* copyright, 1997, United States Catholic Conference, Inc. –Liberia Editrice Vaticana.

Quotations from Vatican Council II are given from <u>Vatican Council II The Conciliar and Post Conciliar Documents</u>, General Editor Austin Flannery, O.P., Published by Pillar Books for Costello Publishing Company, Northport, New York, First printing, November 1975.

[2] One must be careful not to misunderstand this text. The Jewish high priests offered sacrifices repeatedly, both for their own sins as well as for the sins of the people. As is clear from the first and third sentences of this text itself (as well as from elsewhere), Jesus had no "sins of his own" for which to offer sacrifice. Moreover he did not offer himself repeatedly, but rather he offered himself only once and that was for the sins of all people. In the second sentence of this Scripture passage, therefore, the phrase, "first for his own sins" refers, not to

Jesus but only to the other high priests; and the words, "he did that" refer only to the one offering which Jesus made for "the sins of the people," not to any offering for himself.

3 Quoted from The Summa Theologica of St. Thomas Aquinas, First Complete American Edition in three volumes; literally translated by Fathers of the English Dominican Province; volume two, page 2284; Benziger Brothers, Inc. New York, Boston, Cincinnati, Chicago, San Francisco, 1947.

4 "In the Eucharist the Church is as it were at the foot of the cross with Mary, united with the offering and intercession of Christ." (*Catechism of the Catholic Church* #1370)

5 Consider the following passages found in Church documents:
"As often as the sacrifice of the cross by which 'Christ our Pasch is sacrificed'
(1 Cor. 5:7) is celebrated on the altar, the work of our redemption is carried out."
(**Dogmatic Constitution on the Church Vatican II,** *Lumen* *Gentium***, 21 November, 1964, no. 3; Flannery, Vol. 1, pg. 351; see footnote 1 above)**
"When the Church celebrates the Eucharist, she commemorates Christ's Passover, and it is made present: the sacrifice of Christ offered once for all on the cross remains ever present. (Cf. Heb. 7:25-27)" (**Catechism of the Catholic Church # 1364**)
"It is highly fitting that Christ should have wanted to remain present to his Church in this unique way. Since Christ was about to take his departure from his own in his visible form, he wanted to give us his sacramental presence; since he was about to offer himself on the cross to save us, he wanted us to have the memorial of the love with which he loved us "to the end," (Jn. 13:1) even to the giving of his life. In his Eucharistic presence he remains mysteriously in our midst as the one who loved us and gave himself up for us (Cf. Gal 2:20), and he remains under signs that express and communicate this love..."
(**Catechism of the Catholic Church #1380**)
"The Eucharist is above all else a sacrifice. It is the sacrifice of the Redemption and also the sacrifice of the New Covenant, as we believe and as the Eastern Churches clearly profess: 'Today's sacrifice,' the

Greek Church stated centuries ago, 'is like that offered once by the Only Begotten Incarnate Word; it is offered by Him (now as then), since it is one and the same sacrifice.' " **(Dominicae Cenae: On the Mystery and Worship of the Eucharist, # 9,** by His Holiness Pope Saint John Paul II, Promulgated on February 24, 1980**)**

[6] In chapter four (beginning on p. 57), we will consider at greater length the relationship between receiving Holy Communion and our ratifying of the New Covenant.

[7] "Taking part in the Eucharistic sacrifice, the source and summit of the Christian life, they offer the divine victim to God and themselves along with it. And so it is that, both in the offering and in Holy Communion, each in his own way, though not of course indiscriminately, has his own part to play in the liturgical action. Then, strengthened by the body of Christ, in the eucharistic communion, they manifest in a concrete way that unity of the People of God which this holy sacrament aptly signifies and admirably realizes." (Dogmatic Constitution on the Church Vatican II, *Lumen Gentium,* no. 11; Flannery, Vol. 1, pg. 362; see footnote 1 above)

Pope Benedict XVI celebrates the Eucharist at the canonization of Frei Galvão in São Paulo, Brazil on 11 May 2007, courtesy of Wikimedia, https://commons.wikimedia.org/wiki/File:BentoXVI-51-11052007_(frag).jpg

CHAPTER THREE

THE EUCHARISTIC PRAYERS

The Foregoing Theology of the Eucharist Is Expressed in the Four Ordinary Eucharistic Prayers and in the Words of Consecration Prayed During the Mass

In this chapter, I would like to reflect on the words that the celebrant prays, especially in connection with the Consecration of the Mass, in Eucharistic Prayers I, II, III, and IV. We shall see that each of these prayers expresses and confirms the theology of the Eucharist which I set forth in Chapter Two. We will also see that the Words of Consecration themselves imply this theology. In the next chapter, I will present a more complete and detailed reflection on the wording of these Eucharistic Prayers and what they reveal to us about our participation in the celebration of the Mass. In both chapters there will necessarily be some repetition, since we will be considering the same theology of the Eucharist that has already been seen, as we now see it expressed through the words of each of the four ordinary Eucharistic Prayers, along with the Words of Consecration.

[Note: As you read through chapters 3 and 4, should you wish to consult the full text of any of the four ordinary Eucharistic Prayers, you will find them given, for your reference, in Appendix III, beginning on page 145.]

Let us begin with Eucharistic Prayer III, because it most clearly and repeatedly confirms what I have said about the presence of Christ on the altar after the Consecration of the Mass. Immediately after the Consecration, the celebrant invites the congregation to respond to the miracle of Jesus' presence on the altar with those words which are so true,

The mystery of Faith!

The people, in turn, respond in one of three possible prayers:

    A. *We proclaim your Death, O Lord, and profess your Resurrection*
       Until you come again. Or
    B. *When we eat this Bread and drink this Cup, we proclaim your Death,*
       O Lord, until you come again. Or
    C. *Save us, Savior of the world, for by your Cross and Resurrection*
       You have set us free.

Notice that all three of the possible responses clearly refer to <u>the death of Jesus on the cross</u>, although in response C the reference is less explicit than it is in A and B. Next the celebrant prays:

*Therefore, O Lord, as we celebrate the memorial of the **saving Passion of your Son**, his wondrous Resurrection, and Ascension into heaven, and as we look forward to his second coming, we offer you in thanksgiving **this holy and living sacrifice**.*

The celebrant's prayer makes reference to "the saving Passion" of Jesus, which necessarily includes his Death (along with references to his Resurrection and Ascension). Then the celebrant says that we are offering God "this holy and <u>living</u> sacrifice." The sacrifice is living because it is the same continuing Sacrifice of Jesus in love and obedience on Calvary! On the altar He still has the sentiments which made his Death redemptive. It is also "living" insofar as we are offering ourselves in union with Jesus.

The next prayer of the celebrant is even more specific. The celebrant prays:

*Look, we pray, upon the **oblation** of your Church, and **recognizing the sacrificial victim by whose death** you willed to reconcile us to yourself, grant that we who are nourished by the Body and Blood of your Son and filled with his Holy Spirit, may become one body, one spirit in Christ.*

The celebrant is asking God to look upon what is happening on the altar of the Mass, with the Real Presence of Jesus brought about there by the words of Consecration over the bread and wine, and to recognize his Real Presence in the consecrated Host and consecrated Wine as the "sacrificial Victim by whose death" God has willed to reconcile us to Himself. What could be a more explicit statement attesting to the fact that Jesus is now present on the altar with the same essential and necessary sentiments of total love and obedience which, as St. Thomas teaches, made his Death on Calvary redemptive for us? And since Jesus is here with these same sentiments, are we not, then, in a very true sense, miraculously present *At Mass with Jesus on Calvary;* that is, present with him in the continuing, eternal moment of his act of redemption?

In the light of this, the celebrant continues his prayer by asking for unity among those who share in the Body and Blood of Jesus. (We will consider the celebrant's prayer for unity more fully in the next chapter.)

As he begins the next part of the prayer, shown below, the celebrant asks that this Jesus who is present with us in the Eucharist *"make of us an eternal offering"* to God. He is asking God that the grace and power of Jesus' total and eternal surrender in love and obedience to His Father may enable us also to offer ourselves eternally to God, along with Jesus:

> *May he **make of us** an eternal **offering** to you, so that we may obtain an inheritance with your elect, especially with the most Blessed Virgin Mary, Mother of God, with blessed Joseph, her Spouse, with your blessed Apostles and glorious Martyrs (with Saint N.) and with all the Saints, on whose constant intercession in your presence we rely for unfailing help.*

The celebrant makes a final reference to Christ's Eucharistic Presence on the altar as being one with his redeeming death on Calvary when he prays the words,

> *"May this **Sacrifice of our reconciliation**, we pray O Lord, advance the peace and salvation of all the world . . ."*
Again, "This Sacrifice" is the Sacrifice of Calvary, to which we are so intimately joined in the celebration of the Sacrifice of the Mass.

Now let us look at Eucharistic Prayer II

In Eucharistic Prayer II, as in all the other Eucharistic Prayers, immediately after the Consecration, the celebrant invites the congregation to respond to the miracle of Jesus' presence on the altar. The people, in turn, respond, as we saw above (p. 40) for Eucharistic Prayer III, using one of the three prayers containing a reference to the death of Jesus on the cross. The celebrant then prays:

*Therefore, as we celebrate **the memorial of his Death** and Resurrection, we offer you, Lord, the Bread of life and the Chalice of salvation, giving thanks that you have held us worthy **to be in your presence** and minister to you.*

Notice that both the congregation's prayer and the celebrant's prayer—which are prayed immediately after Jesus becomes present on the altar—focus on the death of Jesus: we proclaim his Death; we address him as Savior of the world by reason of his Cross. We celebrate the memorial of his Death. And so these prayers point to the fact that Jesus is present on the altar with the same sentiments of total love and obedience with which he redeemed us by his death on Calvary.

Let's take a closer us look at the celebrant's prayer. It expresses four related thoughts: first, we celebrate the memorial of Jesus' death and resurrection; next we offer God the Bread of life and the Chalice of salvation, which have now become Jesus in his Eucharistic presence; thirdly, we thank God for letting us be in his presence; finally, we thank God also for letting us minister to him.

Again, notice that it is immediately after Jesus becomes present on the altar through the words of Consecration that the celebrant thanks God for allowing us to be in his presence. Moreover, the celebrant expresses this gratitude at the same time "as we celebrate the memorial of his death (and Resurrection)" and "we offer you, Lord, the Bread of Life and the Chalice of Salvation."

Given this context, do not the words "to be in your presence" take on a very special and deep meaning? Are we not here thanking God, not simply for being in his presence as we always are, but especially because we are now in the Eucharistic presence of Jesus with his sentiments of total love and obedience to God which redeemed us on Calvary and which continue at this moment of the Mass and forever? Because we are with Jesus in his action of redemption, are we not thanking God, for letting us, through this marvelous gift, be *At Mass with Jesus on Calvary?*

And now, "on Calvary," along with Jesus and by the help of God's grace, let us offer ourselves to the Father, joining our own limited sentiments of love and obedience to the eternal sentiments of total love and obedience of Jesus. And as we do so, we thank God for enabling us, by this surrender of ourselves, "to minister" to him. (We will consider more fully how we "minister" to God in the next chapter, when we reflect at greater length on these Eucharistic Prayers.)

Next let us look at Eucharistic Prayer IV

Eucharistic Prayer IV is not as explicit in identifying the Presence of Jesus on the altar with the moment of his crucifixion. However, when we reflect on several of its parts taken together, we can see that it does indeed express such an identity.

Just before the words of Consecration the celebrant prays:

> *Therefore O Lord, we pray: may this same Holy Spirit graciously sanctify these offerings that they may become* **the body and blood** *of our Lord Jesus Christ for the celebration of this great mystery,* **which he himself left us as an eternal covenant.**

Remember that the very words Jesus used in instituting the Eucharist indicated that he was giving us his body which, on the following day, would be given up for us in death along with his blood of the new covenant sacrifice. Moreover, when he becomes present on the altar through the words of Consecration, he brings with him the continuing sentiments of love and obedience which he had at the time of his death on Calvary. And so the celebrant prays, "may this same Holy Spirit graciously sanctify these offerings that they may become the body and blood of our Lord Jesus Christ for the celebration of this great mystery, which he himself left us as an eternal covenant." After the words of Consecration, the congregation responds by "proclaiming his death." These words of Eucharistic Prayer IV, then, do reflect the fact that Jesus becomes present on the altar with the eternal sentiments of his redeeming death.

Next the celebrant prays:

*Therefore, O Lord, as we now celebrate the **memorial of our redemption, we remember Christ's Death** and his descent to the realm of the dead, we proclaim his Resurrection and his Ascension to your right hand, and, as we await his coming in glory, **we offer you his Body and Blood, the sacrifice** acceptable to you which brings salvation to the whole world.*

When the celebrant prays, "as we now celebrate the memorial of our redemption, we remember Christ's Death..." and "we offer you his Body and Blood, the sacrifice acceptable to you which brings salvation to the whole world," he is referring explicitly to the death of Jesus on Calvary. The "Body and Blood" we offer is Jesus present on the altar. Again we see clearly that Jesus has become present on the altar with the continuing sentiments of his redeeming death.

The celebrant continues:

*Look, O Lord, upon the **Sacrifice which you yourself***

*have provided for your Church, and grant in your loving kindness to all who partake of this one Bread and one Chalice that, gathered into one body by the Holy Spirit they may truly **become a living sacrifice in Christ** to the praise of your glory.*

God himself has provided the Sacrifice for his Church precisely through Jesus' institution of the Eucharist in relation to his death on Calvary. The Sacrifice which the celebrant now asks God to look upon, then, is the redeeming death of Jesus on Calvary now made present on the altar in the Mass through the celebrant's words of Consecration over the bread and wine.

Moreover, in praying to God to "grant...that they may truly become a living sacrifice in Christ to the praise of your glory," the celebrant is again asking God to enable us truly, through our active participation in the Mass, to join our own self-offering in love and obedience to the sentiments of love and obedience with which Jesus surrendered himself to death in his Sacrifice on Calvary. God has provided the Sacrifice of Jesus and His Presence in the Eucharist. It is up to us, responding to God's grace, to provide in return our self-offering to God.

Finally we examine Eucharistic Prayer I

In Eucharistic Prayer I, also, the presence of Jesus on the altar in the continuing action of his redeeming death and with his eternal sentiments of love and obedience, is expressed when the congregation proclaims that presence in one of the three formulas we saw at the beginning of this chapter (p. 39). In the prayer of the celebrant afterwards, this presence of Jesus in the continuing action of his redeeming death seems to be expressed somewhat more subtly than it is in the other Eucharistic Prayers. Nevertheless, if we reflect carefully, we do see it expressed in the words the celebrant prays after the people's proclamation:

> *Therefore, O Lord,* **as we celebrate the memorial of the blessed Passion,** *the Resurrection from the dead, and the glorious Ascension into heaven of Christ, your Son, our Lord, we, your servants and your holy people, offer to your glorious majesty from the gifts that you have given us,* **this pure victim, this holy victim, this spotless victim, the holy Bread of eternal life and the chalice of everlasting salvation.**

When the celebrant remarks (words in bold) that "we celebrate the memorial of the blessed Passion" and we offer to God "this pure victim, this holy victim, this spotless victim, the holy Bread of eternal life and the chalice of everlasting salvation," he is referring to Christ, the victim, in his redeeming death on Calvary, the summit of his Passion, which he accepted with total love and obedience.

Finally, in the next part of the prayer (below), the celebrant asks God "to look upon these offerings"—namely the Body and Blood of Christ—as "a holy sacrifice, a spotless victim," again a reference to the loving and obedient death of Jesus on the Cross:

Be pleased to look upon these offerings *with a serene and kindly countenance, and to accept them, as once you were pleased to accept the gifts of your servant Abel the just, the sacrifice of Abraham, our father in faith, and the offering of your high priest Melchizedek,* **a holy sacrifice, a spotless victim.**

We have now seen how all four ordinary Eucharistic Prayers express the theology of the Eucharist which I presented in chapter two: namely that what comes about on the altar during Mass is the real, true, and substantial presence of the one and only Jesus, with his same sentiments of total love and obedience which made his death on Calvary redemptive for the whole human race. And Jesus becomes present this way so that we, in a very true sense, can be present with him in this enduring moment of our redemption to offer ourselves to God along with Jesus with as much love and obedience as we can awaken within ourselves at the time.

This same theology of the Eucharist is also expressed in the wording of other optional Eucharistic Prayers (as well as in other prayers of the Mass) although I have limited my commentary to Eucharistic Prayers I, II, III, and IV. Moreover, it is also found in a number of Church documents.[1]

The Words of Consecration

Before concluding this chapter, however, we must also carefully examine the Words of Consecration themselves, which are spoken by the celebrant of the Mass, and which actually bring about the presence of the redeeming Jesus on the altar. For these very words spoken by Jesus himself also point to the theology of the Eucharist which I have presented.

First, consider the actual words of Consecration as they are found in the *Roman Missal* (as given in E.P. II). I will capitalize the actual Words of Consecration prayed over the bread and the wine. I will italicize the words which introduce these words of Consecration, as follows:

At the time he was betrayed and entered willingly into his Passion, he took bread and, giving thanks, broke it, and gave it to his disciples, saying:

TAKE THIS, ALL OF YOU, AND EAT OF IT, FOR THIS IS MY BODY, WHICH WILL BE GIVEN UP FOR YOU.

In a similar way, when supper was ended, he took the chalice and, once more giving thanks, he gave it to his disciples, saying:

TAKE THIS, ALL OF YOU, AND DRINK FROM IT, FOR THIS IS THE CHALICE OF MY BLOOD, THE BLOOD OF THE NEW AND ETERNAL COVENANT, WHICH WILL BE POURED OUT FOR YOU AND FOR MANY FOR THE FORGIVENESS OF SINS. DO THIS IN MEMORY OF ME.

Notice that the words of Jesus spoken at the Last Supper, as indicated by St. Luke's account, and now prayed in the Words of Consecration at Mass are, "This is my Body which will be given up for you." In saying these latter words, Jesus is referring to the crucifixion and death of his body which will take place the following day on Calvary. Thus Jesus specifically relates the institution of the Eucharist to his approaching and redeeming death.

Next, based upon St. Matthew's account, in changing the wine into Jesus' Blood, the celebrant echoes the words of Jesus, "This is the chalice of my blood, the blood of the new and eternal covenant, which will be poured out for you and for many for the forgiveness of sins." Again, the words of Jesus relate the Eucharistic Presence of His Blood to his approaching crucifixion and death.

In addition, when Jesus concludes the institution of the Eucharist with the words, "Do this in memory of me," it seems that in giving us his body and blood in the Eucharist it was his intention actually to extend the redeeming moment of his coming death on Calvary down through the centuries; so that Christians—and particularly Catholics —of each new generation in human history could be immediately present with him, to offer themselves to God in union with Jesus in the sacrifice of himself, which brings about redemption for all mankind and offers the fruit of that redemption to all who will accept it. It is precisely in our wholehearted and conscious participation in the celebration of the Mass that we unite ourselves with this total surrender of Jesus to God, which began on Calvary and continues down through the ages of time and for all eternity.

But let us examine these words of Consecration even further. What does it mean to say that the blood of Jesus is "the blood of the new and eternal covenant"?

The definition of <u>covenant</u> is: "a formal, solemn, and binding agreement." In the Old Testament, the whole history of God's revelation to his Chosen People involved the making of covenants.

Perhaps the most famous covenant made by God after the time of Adam and Eve, was his covenant with Abraham. A few centuries later this covenant was renewed with Moses for God's Chosen People as they were led out of Egypt; and they were to renew it annually down through the centuries at the time of the Passover. However, the People of Israel repeatedly violated their covenant with God. And so it had to be renewed by succeeding Jewish leaders and their people down through the centuries until, hundreds of years later, the prophet Jeremiah announced that in the future God would establish a new (and eternal) covenant.[2]

And just as the earlier covenants with God were established and accepted by his People through the shedding of blood with the sacrifice of animal victims, so the new and eternal covenant would be established the day after the institution of the Eucharist by the blood, not of an animal, but of Jesus himself, bleeding from the cross. This, then, is the meaning of the Words of Consecration, "the blood of the new and eternal covenant."

St. Paul speaks of this in his letter to the Colossians: "It pleased God to make absolute fullness reside in him (Christ Jesus) and, by means of him, to reconcile everything in his person both on earth and in the heavens, making peace through the blood of his cross." (**Col. 1, 19-20**)

We read also in the Letter to the Hebrews, "But when Christ

came as high priest of the good things which have come to be, he entered once for all into the sanctuary, passing through the greater and more perfect tabernacle not made by hands, that is, not belonging to this creation. He entered, not with the blood of goats and calves, but with his own blood, and achieved eternal redemption." **(Hebrews 9, 11-12)**

And so, it is Jesus Himself, in the very words and actions of instituting the Eucharist, who tells us that his real presence on the altar—Body and Blood, soul and divinity—enables us, miraculously, to be present with Him in his very act of redeeming us on Calvary.3

I cannot say it too often: what a magnificent and most marvelous gift our God has given us in the Real Presence of Jesus in the Eucharist!

Endnotes for Chapter 3

¹ 1. Consider again the following examples of Church documents from which I quoted, but not as fully, in the Footnotes for Chapter Two:

Dogmatic Constitution on the Church Vatican II, *Lumen Gentium*, 21 November, 1964; Flannery, Vol.1, pg. 351; see footnote 1, pg. 35.

3. The Son, accordingly, came, sent by the Father who, before the foundation of the world, chose us and predestined us in him for adoptive sonship. For it is in him that it pleased the Father to restore

all things (cf. Eph. 1:4-5 and 10). To carry out the will of the Father Christ inaugurated the kingdom of heaven on earth and revealed to us his mystery; by his obedience he brought about our redemption. The Church—that is the kingdom of Christ—already present in mystery, grows visibly through the power of God in the world. The origin and growth of the Church are symbolized by the blood and water which flowed from the open side of the crucified Jesus (cf. Jn. 19:34), and are foretold in the words of the Lord referring to his death on the cross: "And I, if I be lifted up from the earth, will draw all men to myself" (Jn. 12:32; Gk). As often as the sacrifice of the cross by which "Christ our Pasch is sacrificed" (1 Cor. 5:7) is celebrated on the altar, the work of our redemption is carried out. Likewise, in the sacrament of the eucharistic bread, the unity of believers, who form one body in Christ (cf. 1 Cor. 10:17), is both expressed and brought about. All men are called to this union with Christ, who is the light of the world, from whom we go forth, through whom we live, and towards whom our whole life is directed.

Catechism of the Catholic Church

 # 1364 In the New Testament, the memorial takes on a new meaning. When the Church celebrates the Eucharist, she commemorates Christ's Passover, and it is made present: the sacrifice of Christ offered once for all on the cross remains ever present.
(Cf. Heb. 7:25-27). "As often as the sacrifice of the Cross by which 'Christ our Pasch has been sacrificed' is celebrated on the altar, the work of our redemption is carried out." (LG 3; cf. 1 Cor. 5:7)

 # 1370 To the offering of Christ are united not only the members still here on earth, but also those already *in the glory of heaven*. In communion with and commemorating the Blessed Virgin Mary and all the saints, the Church offers the Eucharistic sacrifice. In the Eucharist the Church is as it were at the foot of the cross with Mary, united with the offering and intercession of Christ.

#1380 It is highly fitting that Christ should have wanted to remain present to his Church in this unique way. Since Christ was about to take his departure from his own in his visible form, he wanted to give us his sacramental presence; since he was about to offer himself on the cross to save us, he wanted us to have the memorial of the love with which he loved us "to the end," (Jn.13:1) even to the giving of his life. In his Eucharistic presence he remains mysteriously in our midst as the one who loved us and gave himself up for us (Cf. Gal 2:20), and he remains under signs that express and communicate this love ... .

[2] **Jeremiah**'s prophecy is given in **chapter 31, verses 31-34**: "The days are coming, says the Lord, when I will make a new covenant with the house of Israel and the house of Judah. It will not be like the covenant I made with their fathers the day I took them by the hand to lead them forth from the land of Egypt; for they broke my covenant, and I had to show myself their master, says the Lord. But this is the covenant which I will make with the house of Israel after those days, says the Lord. I will place my law within them, and write it upon their hearts; I will be their God and they shall be my people. No longer will they have need to teach their friends and kinsmen how to know the Lord. All, from the least to greatest shall know me, says the Lord, for I will forgive their evildoing and remember their sin no more."

Also, in the following chapter, **Jeremiah, 32: 40**, God says, "I will make with them an eternal covenant...."

[3] It should be noted that the Words of Consecration used at Mass, which do quote the actual words of Jesus as given in Scripture (especially "This is my Body" and "This is my Blood"), are a combination, a weaving together, of the words of Jesus from the four separate accounts of the institution of the Eucharist that are given by Matthew, Mark, Luke, and St. Paul (See texts below). Moreover, as happens regularly in the synoptic Gospels, these specific accounts of the institution of the Eucharist show variations in the way Jesus spoke as he instituted the Eucharist, although they all have basically the same meaning. The Words of Consecration used in the Mass, then, which follow closely the words of Scripture and unquestionably express the truth spoken by Jesus at the Last Supper about his Body and his Blood, do not express this truth in exactly the same way it is expressed in any one of the particular accounts found in Scripture.

This is quite understandable considering the fact that the four Scriptural accounts show differences among themselves, although they in no way contradict one another. In the Mass, then, it seems more fitting to combine them rather than to limit the Words of Consecration to just one of the four varying accounts.

Let us examine more carefully the four Scripture accounts which describe the institution of the Holy Eucharist, as they appear in the First Edition (1970) of *The New American Bible*. The words in these accounts which are actually used in the formula for the Words of Consecration during Mass are italicized in bold print.

MATTHEW 26, 26-30

During the meal Jesus took bread, blessed it, broke it, and gave it to his disciples. ***"Take this and eat it,"*** he said, ***"this is my body."*** Then he took the cup, gave thanks, and gave it to them. ***"All of you*** must ***drink from it,"*** he said, ***"for this is my blood, the blood of the covenant, to be poured out in behalf of many for the forgiveness of sins.*** I tell you I will not drink this fruit of the vine from now until the day when I drink it new with you in my Father's reign." Then, after singing songs of praise, they walked out to the Mount of Olives.

MARK 14, 22-26

During the meal he took bread, blessed and broke it, and gave it to them. ***"Take this,"*** *he said,* ***"this is my body."*** He likewise took a cup, gave thanks and passed it to them, and they all drank from it. He said to them: ***"This is my blood, the blood of the covenant, to be poured out on behalf of many.*** I solemnly assure you, I will never again drink of the fruit of the vine until the day when I drink it new in the reign of God." After singing songs of praise, they walked out to the Mount of Olives.

LUKE 22, 19-20

Then, taking bread and giving thanks, he broke it and gave it to them, saying*: "This is my body to be given for you. Do this as a remembrance of me."* He did the same with the cup after eating, saying as he did so: *"This is the new covenant in my blood, which will be shed for you."*

I COR. 11, 23-26

I received from the Lord what I handed on to you, namely, that the Lord Jesus on the night in which he was betrayed took bread, and said, *"This is my body, which is for you. Do this in remembrance of me."* In the same way, after the supper, he took the cup, saying, *"This cup is the new covenant in my blood. Do this, whenever you drink it, in remembrance of me."* Every time, then, you eat this bread and drink this cup, you proclaim the death of the Lord until he comes!

Notice, also, that in none of the above Scriptural accounts of the institution of the Eucharist does Jesus use the expression "all of you" when he gives the disciples his body to eat under the form of bread; but in St. Matthew's account Jesus does use the phrase "all of you" when he gives the disciples his blood to drink under the form of wine. So it makes perfect sense for the phrase "all of you" to be included in the Words of Consecration prayed over the bread as well as over the wine.

Furthermore, the word "eternal" in reference to the "new covenant," does not appear in any of the Scriptural accounts of the institution of the Eucharist itself. However, "eternal" does appear in the Letter to the Hebrews, which reflects at great length on the new covenant in Christ's blood. There, in **Hebrews 9, 12**, we read, "He entered, not with the blood of goats and calves, but with his own blood, and achieved **eternal** redemption." Again, in **Hebrews 13, 20-21,** we read: "May the God of peace, who brought up from the dead the great Shepherd of the sheep by the blood of the **eternal** covenant, Jesus the Lord, furnish you with all that is good, that you may do his will." So, again, it is perfectly acceptable in the Words of Consecration at Mass for the word "eternal" to be inserted as part of the phrase, "the blood of the new and eternal covenant."

And so, taken all together, and in the light of the other New Testament texts which are related to the Eucharist, both the various Scriptural accounts of the institution of the Eucharist and the Words of Consecration attributed to Jesus during the Mass, do express the truth of the words spoken by Jesus at the Last Supper and used as the Words of Consecration in the Mass; namely, that Jesus, under the appearances of bread and wine, gives us his body and blood which he sacrificed on Calvary for the forgiveness of the sins of all human beings.

Notice, too, that although both Scripture and the Words of Consecration over the wine use the expression "poured out for many," the word "many" is understood here to refer to all human beings, since the Church teaches that Jesus died for all and that God wills the salvation of all.

Finally, remember that the words of Consecration as we have them are the official English translation from the Latin text of the *Roman Missal, Third Edition*. There are and have been other legitimate English translations of these words. Such translations themselves may differ slightly in their wording but remain accurate and truthful translations of the Latin text. For example, in the *Roman Missal* Jesus' Words of Consecration over the bread are translated, "Take this, all of you, and eat of it, for this is my <u>body, **which will be given up for you**</u>." But in the New American Bible (1ˢᵗ ed.), in St. Luke's Gospel, the words of Jesus are translated, "This is my <u>body **to be given for you**</u>."

CHAPTER FOUR

LOOK CLOSER

Further Reflections on the Eucharistic Prayers

In the previous chapter we have seen how the prayers both of the congregation and of the celebrant, which come just before or after the Consecration of the Mass, reflect the nature of Christ's Eucharistic Presence on the altar. Now it is time to reflect more in detail on each of these four ordinary Eucharistic Prayers.

In these Eucharistic Prayers the words <u>gift</u>, <u>offering</u>, <u>sacrifice</u>, and <u>oblation</u> are used repeatedly.[1] However, while all of these words are similar to one another and can have the same general meaning, careful reflection will show us that, as they appear in various places during the Eucharistic Prayers, the same word does not always have the same meaning each time it is used because it does not always refer to the same reality.

In reflecting on these words, we will come to see that during the Mass we actually offer three related but independent realities to God: we offer bread and wine; we offer Jesus in His Sacrifice on Calvary; we offer ourselves. Let us now examine these various offerings, along with other aspects of the four ordinary Eucharistic Prayers.

Eucharistic Prayer II

Let us begin with Eucharistic Prayer II, since it is the shortest of the four Prayers and the easiest to analyze.

Eucharist Prayer II contains the fewest references to what is offered to God during the Mass. In fact, before the Consecration it makes only one reference to the bread and wine; and, after the Consecration, it makes only one reference to offering Jesus in his Eucharistic Presence to God. It also refers to our "partaking of the Body and Blood of Christ," which is the only other reference this prayer makes to what is on the altar and its relation to those present at the Mass.

At the beginning of this Eucharistic Prayer, the celebrant prays,

You are indeed Holy, O Lord, the fount of all holiness.

*Make holy, therefore, these **gifts**, we pray, by sending down your Spirit upon them like the dewfall, so that they may become for us the Body and Blood of our Lord Jesus Christ.*

Here the word <u>gifts</u> refers to the bread and wine which are on the altar for Consecration. But let us ask the question, "What does it mean to ask God to make the bread and wine <u>holy</u>?" Are they unholy as they rest on the paten* and in the chalice? Is there something defective about them?

Notice that the celebrant continues his request for the holiness of the gifts by praying," *so that they may become for us the Body and Blood of our Lord Jesus Christ.*" Can we not say that God makes them holy by choosing them as the special subjects—this particular bread and wine on the altar; not just any bread and wine wherever it may be found –to be changed by His divine and miraculous power into the Body and Blood of Jesus? And is it not true to say that it is precisely by God's taking away their substances as bread and as wine and joining to their remaining species the substance of the Body and Blood of Jesus that the bread and wine will become the holiness of God Himself?

In other words, it seems it is because of their relationship to the approaching Consecration that the priest speaks of their being made holy by God. And after the Consecration, of course, there will no longer be, in substance, any bread or wine on the altar, but only their appearances.

After the words of Consecration, as we saw in chapter three, the celebrant invites the congregation to acknowledge this marvelous mystery of our faith. After the congregation proclaims the Death of Jesus, the celebrant continues,

*Therefore, as we celebrate the memorial of his Death and Resurrection, we **offer** you, Lord, the **Bread of life** and the **Chalice of salvation**, giving thanks that you have held us worthy to be in your presence and **minister to you.***

In this prayer, the celebrant says that, together with the congregation, he is offering to God what is now on the altar, no longer bread and wine, but Jesus Himself, whom the celebrant refers to as the "Bread of life" and the "Chalice of salvation." Then he thanks God for allowing us to be in his presence and minister to him.

Once again, we must reflect more deeply on the meaning of these words, which we have already considered briefly in the previous chapter. Since what is now present on the altar is Jesus Himself in the eternal moment of his Sacrifice on Calvary, that is, with his sentiments of love and obedience in accepting death for our salvation, has he not already offered himself to the Father at the moment of death and does he not continue to do so for all eternity? What then, can it mean for the priest, in our name, to tell God that <u>we</u> offer to him His Son's sacrifice? The Sacrifice itself of Jesus is his to offer, not ours. We cannot take any credit for it. And he has already offered it over 2000 years ago. What, then, do the celebrant's words mean?

Well, there are at least two things they can mean. First of all, we can "be happy about," or "in favor of" what Jesus has done for us. To put it in the language of legislators, we can "second the motion" of his redeeming sacrifice. In this sense, we can truly say that "we offer" to God "the Bread of Life and the Chalice of salvation." Secondly, and more importantly for us, at this sacred moment of the Mass we can, so to speak, become partners with Jesus, by offering ourselves to God in union with the Sacrifice of Jesus.

After all, if we are "just there" at Mass and nothing else, what good is it? Remember, the presence of Jesus on the altar does nothing more to advance our salvation beyond what he has already done on Calvary and in interceding for us at the right hand of his Father—except to give us this very special opportunity to respond to what he has done. And how can our response be meaningful if it does not include our own self-offering in union with Jesus? The reason He is there is so that his saving presence can have its effect on us. But this necessarily requires a willing acceptance on our part. And how can there be any acceptance of, or entering into, the redeeming action of Jesus in our lives if it does not involve our embracing his saving death and joining him in the sentiments of love and obedience by which he wants to redeem us? What else is there that can be worthwhile or meaningful in our reaction to his Eucharistic Presence, if it does not include our own self-surrender, along with Jesus, in love and obedience to the Father? As I said earlier, it is not a question of what we "get out" of the Mass, but of what we "put into" it, so that being at Mass will be of little or no benefit to us unless we bring our own self-offering to it.

Jesus has brought his "once for all" **(Heb. 7:28)** redeeming death to the altar at Mass. And now is the moment for us to accept his saving gift by offering our lives to God along with Jesus as he offers Himself in total obedience "even unto death on a cross." And when God sees that we are making our self-offering in union with the self-offering of His Son Jesus, it will make our offering all the more pleasing to God. The next words prayed by the celebrant, indeed, can be understood as our thanking God for this opportunity to offer ourselves to Him along with the total self-offering of Jesus:

*"giving thanks that you have held us worthy to be in your presence and **minister* to you.**"*

How do we "minister"* to God? God is in no need whatsoever of any ministry from us. There is nothing we can do to add to God's already infinite perfection. He needs absolutely nothing from us. So again I ask, what does it mean to say that we "minister" to God? It means that in this sacred moment we give ourselves to God as fully as we can. It means that we will always try to please God by what we do in our daily lives. To "minister to God" means to offer ourselves to Him, along with Jesus, as completely as we can. And, of course, it is we ourselves, not God, who benefit from our "ministering" to God in this way.

In the remainder of Eucharistic Prayer II the celebrant asks God for several different things. First he prays for unity among ourselves:

*Humbly we pray that, partaking of the Body and Blood of Christ, **we may be gathered into one by the Holy Spirit.***

And notice that it is especially by the fact that we all share the same Body and Blood of Christ in Holy Communion that we are brought into closer unity with one another; and so the celebrant prays, further, that the Holy Spirit may strengthen this unity and help us to realize it and live according to it. (I'll say more about this unity later on.)

It is good to recall here, too, what I mentioned briefly in chapter two about "sacrifice" and the receiving of Holy Communion (p. 34). Remember that in some of the ancient Jewish sacrifices to God the people showed their approval and participation in the covenant-sacrifice by eating, in a post-sacrificial meal, some of the victim which had been offered. When we receive Holy Communion, we eat Christ's body and drink his blood, that is, we are eating of the victim of the Sacrifice of the Mass; and so this becomes a sign of our acceptance of, and our commitment to live according to, the "new and eternal covenant" made with God through the sacrificial death of Jesus.

Receiving Holy Communion, then, should not be a routine, pious action which we perform casually near the end of the Mass. Rather, when we receive Holy Communion, we should again offer ourselves to God in union with those sentiments of total self-surrender in love and obedience to God, with which Jesus died on Calvary; sentiments which he continues to possess as he comes within us, and will possess for all eternity. Our reception of Holy Communion should be the sign of our profound affirmation of the Sacrifice of Jesus, to which we have joined our own self-offering in the Mass.

Even more profound and marvelous, of course, is the fact that not only has Jesus offered His life for us, but in Holy Communion he comes within us as our food and drink in an intimate act of love and friendship which is unparalleled anywhere else in our human experience.

As the celebrant continues Eucharistic Prayer II, he asks God to bring about the fullness of his love in his Church and its hierarchy throughout the world.

Remember, Lord, your Church, spread throughout the world, and bring her to the fullness of charity, together with N. our Pope and N. our Bishop and all the clergy.

Then he asks God to welcome into heaven all those who have died in his mercy, especially those who have died in the hope of Christ's Resurrection.

Remember also our brothers and sisters who have fallen asleep in the hope of the resurrection, and all who have died in your mercy: welcome them into the light of your face.

In Masses for the Dead, the above prayer is immediately preceded by a prayer that the deceased person, united with Christ in death, might share in his Resurrection.

Finally, the celebrant prays for God's mercy on everyone so that all of us may join Mary and Joseph and the Apostles of her Son and all the Saints in the eternal life of heaven, praising God through Jesus Christ.

Have mercy on us all, we pray, that with the Blessed Virgin Mary, Mother of God, with blessed Joseph, her Spouse, with the blessed Apostles, and all the Saints who have pleased you throughout the ages, we may merit to be coheirs* to eternal life, and may praise and glorify you through your Son, Jesus Christ.

Like all the other Eucharistic Prayers, Eucharistic Prayer II ends with a solemn proclamation that God, Who is Father, Son, and Holy Spirit, receives all glory and honor from human beings on earth through the incarnate Son, Jesus Christ.

Through him, and with him, and in him, O God, almighty Father, in the unity of the Holy Spirit, all glory and honor is yours, for ever and ever. Amen.

Notice that the above words are not simply the usual way of ending a prayer by saying that we are praying "through our Lord Jesus Christ," thus invoking his intercession for us before the Father. Rather, these words at the end of every Eucharistic Prayer are the solemn proclamation and powerful declaration of the supremacy of the man-God Jesus Christ, through whom all honor and glory of any and every sort are given to God from all the human race (and even from the angels).

Eucharistic Prayer I

Now let us look more closely at Eucharistic Prayer I. After the "Holy, Holy, Holy" the priest begins Eucharistic Prayer I by praying,

*To you, therefore, most merciful Father, we make humble prayer and petition through Jesus Christ, your Son, our Lord: that you accept and bless these **gifts**, these **offerings**, these holy and unblemished **sacrifices**, **which** we offer you firstly for your holy catholic Church. Be pleased to grant her peace, to guard, unite and govern her throughout the whole world, together with your servant N. our Pope and N. our Bishop, and all those who, holding to the truth, hand on the catholic and apostolic faith.*

In the above prayer, the words (in bold) <u>gifts</u>, <u>offerings</u>, <u>sacrifices</u>, and <u>which</u> all refer to the bread and wine which are present on the altar for consecration into the body and blood of

Jesus. The celebrant indicates this by making the sign of the cross over them as he prays the words. Of course, there are many ways in which the bread and wine on the altar can be considered as "gifts." They are first of all gifts of God to all people on earth. The celebrant, in fact, acknowledges this earlier in the Mass, during the preparation of the gifts, when he prays, "Blessed are you, Lord God of all creation, for through your goodness we have received the bread (and wine) we offer you." Elsewhere, too, the prayers of the Mass speak of all God's gifts to us. The bread and wine on the altar over which the celebrant now prays the above Eucharistic Prayer are called "gifts" more specifically in the sense that, after having been made from wheat and grapes by human hands, they have been afterwards bought and provided for the Eucharistic celebration through the donations of the members of the parish where the Mass is being celebrated; even more importantly, they are called "gifts" because the celebrant is actually offering them to God. They are also called "offerings" for this same reason. They will become "sacrifices" only when they are changed into the Body and Blood of Jesus by the words of Consecration.

In fact, it is only in relation to this change into the Body and Blood of Christ that the priest and congregation can sincerely offer the bread and wine to God. When we consider all of God's many magnificent gifts to us in our own existence and in all of creation; and considering all the possibilities of what we actually have available to offer, surely it would not be an appropriate offering to God, nor worthy of ourselves, for us to offer Him only a few wafers of bread and a few ounces of wine. But remember again that we are not offering the bread and wine to God in themselves, but precisely in relation to their becoming the Body and Blood of His Son, which are, in fact, supremely worthy of being offered to God and totally pleasing to Him.

in the next part of the prayer which the priest prays, he again uses the word <u>sacrifice</u> and the pronoun <u>it</u> in referring back to the word <u>sacrifice</u>:

> *Remember, Lord, your servants N. and N. and all gathered here, whose faith and devotion are known to you. For them, we offer you this* **sacrifice** *of praise or they offer* **it** *for themselves and all who are dear to them: for the redemption of their souls, in hope of health and well-being, and paying their homage to you, the eternal God, living and true.*

Here the word "sacrifice" refers to something more than just the bread and wine on the altar; rather, it refers to the celebration of the Mass as a whole. In fact, as I have already said, the bread and wine do not become an actual sacrifice until the words of Consecration are spoken over them.

Notice, too, in the above prayer, that the priest qualifies the word "sacrifice" as being one "of praise." "Praise" presupposes the words and actions of the celebrant, and even of the congregation. In addition, the celebrant says, "<u>we</u> offer you." And although this could be understood as an editorial use of the word "we," referring to the priest himself, it seems to me that it should rather be understood as referring to both the priest and the congregation, especially since the celebrant immediately continues, "or they offer it for themselves and all who are dear to them."

Insofar as the priest is the only person who brings about the presence of Jesus on the altar through the words of Consecration, it could be said that he alone "offers" "this sacrifice of praise." However, he offers the sacrifice not merely to ask blessings on the congregation but he also offers it precisely as the leader of all who are present, so that the members of the congregation themselves, by their participation in the Mass, may join the celebrant in the offering of this holy sacrifice.

Do not misunderstand. There are not two separate sacrifices, one by the priest and another one by the people. The priest offers the one sacrifice for himself, on behalf of and for the whole congregation, and especially for those mentioned by name; and along with the celebrant all gathered at the Mass "offer it for themselves and all who are dear to them." It is one and the same sacrifice, which reaches its fullness when the priest prays the words of Consecration over the bread and wine. It is then that the primary "Sacrifice" offered in the Mass takes place, namely the offering of the Body and Blood of Christ, in fact, the whole Christ—Body and Blood, soul and divinity—(as the *Decree on the Most Holy Eucharist* says).

But (as we saw in reflecting on Eucharistic Prayer II), since Jesus has already offered himself in sacrifice to God two thousand years ago when he died on Calvary, we see again that, at Mass, the "sacrifice of praise" offered to God by the celebrant and the congregation is their endorsing of this Sacrifice of Jesus and, then, their surrendering of themselves to God along with Jesus. Adoration and petitions are explicitly mentioned as reasons for offering the Sacrifice.

In the next part of the Eucharistic Prayer the celebrant asks God to protect us, invoking the intercession of Mary, St. Joseph, the Apostles, the early Saints in the Church, and all the Saints. Afterwards the celebrant prays the following words:

> *Therefore, Lord, we pray: graciously accept this* **oblation** *of our service, that of your whole family; order our days in your peace, and command that we be delivered from eternal damnation and counted among the flock of those you have chosen. (Through Christ our Lord. Amen.)*

Here the word oblation (like sacrifice above) refers not only to the bread and wine on the altar for consecration, but also to the whole Mass itself, in which, as God's servants, we participate to offer ourselves along with the Holy Sacrifice of Jesus, about to be made present to us in the words of Consecration. And the celebrant adds that this oblation is from "your whole family." A Mass offered by a particular celebrant and congregation any-where in the world is always offered in union with all Catholics all over the world, (not to mention the Souls in Purgatory and the Saints in Heaven). More petitions follow.

Then the priest continues,

*Be pleased, O God, we pray, to bless, acknowledge, and approve this **offering** in every respect; make **it** spiritual and acceptable, so that **it** may become for us the Body and Blood of your most beloved Son, our Lord Jesus Christ.*

Once again, careful reflection on the above words tells us that the word "offering" used here must refer to more than just the bread and wine on the altar. What does it mean for the priest to ask God "to bless, acknowledge, and approve this offering in every respect" and to ask Him to "make it spiritual and acceptable so that it may become for us the Body and Blood of ...Christ"?

As previously stated, there is nothing the matter with the bread and wine itself. It is not in some way imperfect or unacceptable to be used for consecration into the Body and Blood of Christ. But it is we ourselves—the celebrant and the congregation who are offering to God the bread and wine, and especially the Body and Blood of His Son after the words of Consecration –it is our sharing in the offering, our attitude and sentiments as we participate in the Mass, which we ask God to *"bless, acknowledge, and approve"...in every respect."* It is we, who need to be made *"spiritual and acceptable"* in the way we make this offering—above all including the offering of ourselves, along with Jesus, to God. We must be totally sincere, not thoughtlessly routine, in our assisting at the celebration of

Mass.

Both the word <u>offering</u> and the pronoun which follows in the words, *"make <u>it</u> spiritual and acceptable"* refer, then, especially to our self-offering in union with the Self-Offering of Jesus, who will become present with us in the words of Consecration. On the other hand, the second use of the pronoun "it," in the phrase, *"so that <u>it</u> may become for us the Body and Blood"* etc., refers only to the bread and wine on the altar.

Next the celebrant prays the actual words of Consecration, and the acclamation of the people follows. Then the celebrant continues:

> *Therefore, O Lord,* **as we celebrate the memorial of the blessed Passion,** *the Resurrection from the dead, and the glorious Ascension into heaven of Christ, your Son, our Lord, we, your servants and your holy people, offer to your glorious majesty from the* **gifts** *that you have given us,* **this pure victim, this holy victim, this spotless victim, the holy Bread of eternal life and the chalice of everlasting salvation.**

I have already commented on this prayer in the previous chapter (pg. 47). Let me add that here the word "gifts" refers to all God's gifts to people on earth, including the bread and wine which have just been consecrated into the body and blood of Jesus; and so we now include the greatest gift of all *"this pure victim, this holy victim, this spotless victim, the holy Bread of eternal life and the Chalice of everlasting salvation,"* namely, Jesus Himself.

Then the celebrant continues Eucharistic Prayer I by praying,

> *Be pleased to look upon these* **offerings** *with a serene and kindly countenance, and to accept* **them**, *as once you were*

*pleased to accept the gifts of your servant Abel the just, the sacrifice of Abraham, our father in faith, and the offering of your high priest Melchizedek, a holy **sacrifice**, a spotless **victim**.*

As we saw in our reflections on Eucharistic Prayer II, no longer is there bread and wine on the altar, but only their appearances, containing the Body and Blood of Jesus in his Holy Sacrifice. And so, here the word "offerings" refers, first of all, to Jesus who is present in this way. But, as we have also seen, the Self-Offering of Jesus is infinitely perfect, took place long ago, and was accepted by God at that time. Moreover, in his natural way of existing, even now Jesus sits at the right hand of God the Father, face to face, in his eternal Self-Offering.

Therefore, when we ask God to *"be pleased to look upon these offerings with a serene and kindly countenance, and to accept them,"* the word "offerings" must also refer to us. The only thing left for God to accept, as we have seen also before, is our own appreciation of Jesus' offering and the offering of ourselves along with him. Moreover, the references in the prayer to the "gifts of Abel," "the sacrifice of Abraham" and the "offering of your high priest Melchizedek"—whose sacrifices were acceptable to God precisely because of their upright attitudes in offering them—make it clear that it is the sincerity of our own sentiments and attitude in making this offering, which we are again asking God to be pleased with.

Since both the words "sacrifice" and "victim" refer to Jesus in His Eucharistic Presence, the sincerity of the *"spotless victim"* is already guaranteed. But for God *"to accept"* as a *"holy sacrifice"* our offering of that victim along with ourselves on this particular occasion depends, in part, on us. Is our offering honest and sincere? As a matter of fact, without God's grace, we are not able to make a sincere offering of ourselves. It is precisely this grace, then, for which the celebrant is again praying when he asks God to, "*be pleased to look upon these offerings with a serene and kindly countenance, and to accept them,*" as He once accepted the offerings of Abel, Abraham, and Melchizedek.

Next the celebrant prays,

*In humble prayer we ask you, almighty God: command that these **gifts** be borne by the hands of your holy Angel to your altar on high in the sight of your divine majesty, so that all of us, who through this participation at the altar receive the most holy Body and Blood of your Son, may be filled with every grace and heavenly blessing. (Through Christ our Lord. Amen.)*

The word "gifts" here refers both to the offering of Jesus and to the offering of ourselves along with him. Once again, however, we must remember that there is only one Jesus. And, in reality, this one Jesus—who has already made his total, eternal, Self-Offering to God—is already present, in His natural way of existing, at God's "altar on high in the sight of (His) divine majesty." Even the gift of our own self-offering does not need to be carried to heaven for God to be aware of it and accept it. So the first words of this part of the Eucharistic prayer seem to be, not a question of a geographical movement from earth to heaven, but rather a beautiful, poetic way of asking God, once more, to accept what <u>we</u> are doing at Mass. The latter words of the prayer, however, are a practical, here-and-now petition to God, asking that all of us, through our participation at this Mass and the receiving of Holy Communion, "*may be filled with every grace and heavenly blessing.*"

In the remaining parts of Eucharistic Prayer I, we pray for the eternal happiness of those who have died in faith before us. Afterwards we pray for ourselves to someday share heaven with the Apostles, the early martyrs, both men and women, and with all the saints:

Remember also, Lord, your servants N. and N., who have gone before us with the sign of faith and rest in the sleep of peace. Grant them, O Lord, we pray, and all who sleep in Christ, a place of refreshment, light and peace. (Through Christ our Lord. Amen.)

To us, also, your servants, who, though sinners, hope in your abundant mercies, graciously grant some share and fellowship with your holy Apostles and Martyrs: with John the Baptist, Stephen, Matthias, Barnabas, (Ignatius, Alexander, Marcellinus, Peter, Felicity, Perpetua, Agatha, Lucy, Agnes, Cecilia, Anastasia) and all your Saints; admit us, we beseech you, into their company, not weighing our merits, but granting us your pardon, through Christ our Lord.

The celebrant concludes Eucharistic Prayer I first by acknowledging that all God's blessings and gifts, including the Mass we offer, come down to us through Jesus Christ; then, in the proclamation that ends every Eucharistic Prayer he declares also that all glory goes up to God from the earth, through Jesus Christ.

Through whom you continue to make all these good things, O Lord; you sanctify them, fill them with life, bless them, and bestow them upon us.

Through him, and with him, and in him, O God, almighty Father, in the unity of the Holy Spirit, all glory and honor is yours, for ever and ever. Amen.

Eucharistic Prayer III

Eucharistic Prayer III begins as follows:

*You are indeed Holy, O Lord, and all you have created rightly gives you praise, for through your Son our Lord Jesus Christ, by the power and working of the Holy Spirit, you give life to all things and make them holy, and you never cease to gather a people to yourself, so that from the rising of the sun to its setting a pure **sacrifice** may be offered to your name.*

The word <u>sacrifice</u>, as it appears in the opening words of this Eucharistic Prayer has the general meaning of any sacrifice offered to God; but it also refers more specifically to the Sacrifice of the Mass now being offered. By the words of Consecration, this becomes the Sacrifice of Jesus on Calvary. And since the Mass is constantly being offered in Catholic churches all over the world, the celebrant acknowledges to God, "you never cease to gather a people to yourself, so that from the rising of the sun to its setting a pure sacrifice may be offered to your name." Of its very nature this sacrifice of Jesus is "pure" or perfect.

The celebrant continues:

*Therefore, O Lord, we humbly implore you: by the same Spirit graciously make holy these **gifts** we have brought to you for consecration, that they may become the Body and Blood of your Son our Lord Jesus Christ, at whose command we celebrate these mysteries.*

Here the word <u>gifts</u> clearly refers to the bread and wine on the altar. There follows the two-fold part of the Eucharistic Prayer in which the celebrant recites the words of Consecration.

In the previous chapter we have already reflected on the meaning of some parts of Eucharistic Prayer III which follow the words of Consecration and the acclamation of the congregation. Now let us reflect more fully on the celebrant's words:

*Look, we pray, upon the **oblation** of your Church and, recognizing the sacrificial Victim by whose death you willed to reconcile us to yourself, grant that we, who are nourished by the Body and Blood of your Son and filled with his Holy Spirit, **may become one body, one spirit in Christ.***

The oblation which the Church now offers is Jesus himself, the sacrificial victim of Calvary. Our own self-surrender to God in love and obedience, in union with Jesus, should also be included in this oblation.

Next consider the latter half of the above prayer, namely: "grant that we, who are nourished by the Body and Blood of your Son and filled with his Holy Spirit, may become one body, one spirit in Christ."

This prayer to God for unity among the members of his Church is prayed in all four of the ordinary Eucharistic Prayers, as well as during the prayer just before exchanging the sign of peace. In Eucharistic Prayers II, III, and IV, this petition is related to the receiving of Holy Communion and is prominently made during the second short prayer following the acclamation after the Consecration. In Eucharistic Prayer I, it is made briefly, without a reference to Holy Communion, almost at the very beginning of the prayer. These petitions for unity appear as follows:

*E.P.I—Be pleased to grant her peace, to guard, **unite**, and govern her throughout the whole world. . .*

E.P.II—*Humbly we pray that, partaking of the Body and Blood of Christ, we may be **gathered into one** by the Holy Spirit.*

E.P.III—*...grant that we, who are nourished by the Body and Blood of your Son and filled with his Holy Spirit, **may become one body, one spirit** in Christ.*

E.P.IV—*...grant in your loving kindness to all who partake of this one Bread and one Chalice that, **gathered into one body** by the Holy Spirit, they may truly become a living sacrifice in Christ.*

Except for Eucharistic Prayer I, these prayers explicitly express a relationship between the receiving of Holy Communion and the unity of the Church. Let us remember that the Mass is not something we celebrate as individuals, but as a united community; and celebrating it together should always deepen our unity as believing Catholic Christians. In addition, the fact that we all receive the one Jesus in Holy Communion immensely increases our unity. And so, we should make a serious effort to be aware of the unity which is ours in Jesus Christ, a unity for which He prayed so earnestly at the Last Supper after he had instituted the Eucharist:

"I pray also for those who will believe in me through their (the Apostles') word, that all may be one as you, Father, are in me, and I in you; I pray that they may be one in us that the world may believe that you sent me...I living in them, you living in me –that their unity may be complete. So shall the world know that you sent me, and that you loved them as you loved me." **(John 17: 20-21, 23)**

What a powerful prayer of Jesus this is! And what a powerful source of nourishment is his gift of the Eucharist to bring about the unity for which He prayed!

After the request for unity, the celebrant continues,

May he make of us an eternal offering to you, so that we may obtain an inheritance with your elect, especially with the most Blessed Virgin Mary, Mother of God, with blessed Joseph, her Spouse, with your blessed Apostles and glorious Martyrs (with Saint N.) and with all the Saints, on whose constant intercession in your presence we rely for unfailing help.

As I noted in chapter three (pg. 42), the first words of this prayer are an appeal for the grace to offer ourselves to God in union with Jesus. We ask that the making of this self-offering will enable us someday to share heaven with Mary, Mother of God, with St. Joseph, with the Apostles, Martyrs, and all the Saints, especially the patron saint of the parish where the Mass is being offered (and/or the saint of the day), noting that we rely on their constant intercession for us before God.

Then the celebrant continues,

May this Sacrifice of our reconciliation, we pray, O Lord, advance the peace and salvation of all the world. Be pleased to confirm in faith and charity your pilgrim Church on earth, with your servant N. our Pope and N. our Bishop, the Order of Bishops, all the clergy, and the entire people you have gained for your own.

The first words of this prayer, also noted in chapter three, indicate the presence of Jesus on the altar in his act of redemption; and we ask that this presence may foster peace and salvation for the whole world. Then we pray that the Church on earth—which includes the Pope, our own Bishop and all Bishops, all clergy, and all who have become God's People—be confirmed and strengthened in its faith and its charity.

In the final two parts of Eucharistic Prayer III, the celebrant first asks God to listen to the prayers of those who have gathered for the celebration of this Mass and to gather to Himself all his children scattered throughout the world, once again implying the idea of unity.

Listen graciously to the prayers of this family, whom you have summoned before you: in your compassion, O merciful Father, gather to yourself all your children scattered throughout the world.

Next he prays that Catholics and all who have died in God's grace be admitted into heaven, where we hope one day to enjoy forever the fullness of God's glory. He prays through Christ our Lord, declaring that through him God bestows on the world all that is good.

To our departed brothers and sisters and to all who were pleasing to you at their passing from this life, give kind admittance to your kingdom. There we hope to enjoy for ever the fullness of your glory through Christ our Lord, through whom you bestow on the world all that is good.

In the alternate form of this prayer, which is used only in Masses for the Dead and which includes the above words, the celebrant asks God to remember a recently deceased individual; praying that since he (she) has now shared in the death of Jesus, he (she) may, at the final judgment, also share in his Resurrection, when he will raise our bodies and transform them so that they will become like his glorious body. The prayer concludes with the reflection that in heaven all tears will be wiped away because we shall see God as He is and share his being forever in unending praise.

Remember your servant N., whom you have called (today) from this world to yourself. Grant that he (she) who was united with your Son in a death like his, may also be one with him in his Resurrection, when from the earth he will raise up in the flesh those who have died, and transform our lowly body after the pattern of his own glorious body. To our departed brothers and sisters, too, and to all who were pleasing to you at their passing from this life, give kind admittance to your kingdom. There we hope to enjoy for ever the fullness of your glory, when you will wipe away every tear from our eyes. For seeing you, our God, as you are, we shall be like you for all the ages and praise you without end, through Christ our Lord, through whom you bestow on the world all that is good.

Afterwards the celebrant concludes Eucharistic Prayer III with the usual proclamation that all glory from earth reaches God through Jesus.

Eucharistic Prayer IV

Eucharistic Prayer IV is very different from the other three ordinary Eucharistic Prayers. It is much longer, and, in fact, as you can see below, it gives a synoptic account of the whole history of salvation. In chapter three (pp. 44-45) I commented on several parts of this Prayer. Now let us consider it further. It has its own Preface, which speaks of God's eternal being before creation. Following the "Holy, Holy, Holy" the prayer itself begins,

We give you praise, Father most holy, for you are great and

you have fashioned all your works in wisdom and in love. You formed man in your own image and entrusted the whole world to his care, so that in serving you alone, the Creator, he might have dominion over all creatures. And when through disobedience he had lost your friendship, you did not abandon him to the domain of death. For you came in mercy to the aid of all, so that those who seek might find you. **Time and again you offered them covenants** *and through the prophets taught them to look forward to salvation.*

And you so loved the world, Father most holy, that in the fullness of time you sent your Only Begotten* Son to be our Savior. Made incarnate by the Holy Spirit and born of the Virgin Mary, he shared our human nature in all things but sin. To the poor he proclaimed the good news of salvation, to prisoners, freedom, and to the sorrowful of heart, joy. To accomplish your plan, he gave himself up to death, and, rising from the dead, he destroyed death and restored life.

And that we might live no longer for ourselves but for him who died and rose again for us, he sent the Holy Spirit from you, Father, as the first fruits for those who believe, so that, bringing to perfection his work in the world, he might sanctify creation to the full.

Let me make a few simple comments on the lines which are shown above in bold print. First of all, Eucharistic Prayer IV relates more explicitly than the other Eucharistic Prayers to the words of Consecration spoken by Jesus when it says, *"Time and again you offered them covenants..."* Remember that Jesus' words were, *"This is my Blood of the New (and Eternal) Covenant."* The primary covenants which had come before were those made with Abraham and with Moses, as we have seen.

A little further on, the priest prays,

*"And that **we might live no longer for ourselves but for him who died and rose again for us**, he sent **the Holy Spirit** from you, Father, **as the first fruits** for those who believe....*

The preceding words remind us of four of St. Paul's letters. In his Letter to the Galatians, he writes, "It was through the law that I died to the law, to live for God. I have been crucified with Christ, and **the life I live now is not my own; Christ is living in me.** I still live my own human life, but it is a life of faith in the Son of God, who loved me and gave himself for me." **(Gal. 2, 19-20)**

Even more explicitly, St. Paul writes in his Second Letter to the Corinthians, "And he died for all, that those who live **might live no longer for themselves but for him who for their sake died and was raised." (2 Cor. 5, 15)**

In his Letter to the Romans, Paul writes, "...we have the **Spirit as first fruits....**" **(Rm. 8, 23)**

Finally, Paul expresses this idea in his Letter to the Ephesians: "...you were sealed with **the Holy Spirit** who had been promised. He is **the pledge of our inheritance, the first payment** against the full redemption of a people God has made his own, to praise his glory." **(Eph. 1, 13-14)**

In the next chapter, we will see many more examples of how the words used in the Mass are based on passages from Scripture.

Now let us look again briefly at the following words of Eucharistic Prayer IV, which appear shortly before the words of Consecration:

Therefore O Lord, we pray: may this same Holy Spirit

*graciously **sanctify** these **offerings** that they may become the body and blood of our Lord Jesus Christ for the celebration of this great mystery, which he himself left us as **an eternal covenant**.*

Let me simply observe here that in this prayer the word "offerings" refers only to the bread and wine on the altar. The explanation given at the beginning of this chapter (pg. 58) as to what it means for the Holy Spirit to "make holy" the gifts of bread and wine applies also to the words of this prayer, asking that the "Holy Spirit sanctify these offerings." We've seen earlier, too, (pgs. 44-45) what it means for Jesus to leave us the Mass as "an eternal covenant."

After the Words of Consecration the celebrant prays the two parts of Eucharistic Prayer IV on which I commented in chapter three (pgs. 44-45). The celebrant then continues:

*Therefore, Lord, remember now all for whom we offer this **sacrifice**: especially your servant N. our Pope, N. our Bishop, and the whole Order of Bishops, all the clergy, those who take part in this **offering**, those gathered here before you, your entire people, and all who seek you with a sincere heart.*

Here the word "sacrifice" refers both to the redeeming Sacrifice of Jesus now present on the altar and the self-offering of the celebrant and congregation made in union with Jesus. The word "offering" refers to the celebration of the Mass as a whole. And notice that in addition to praying especially for the Pope the local Bishop and all Bishops and clergy, the celebrant says that those for whom the Mass is offered include all those present, all the people of God, and all who seek God with a sincere heart.

Finally, in the last two parts of the prayer, we pray first for all human beings who have died, especially those who have died in the peace of Christ; and we ask that we who are God's children (through Baptism) may be united someday in heaven with the Blessed Virgin Mary, the Apostles, and all the Saints, to glorify God through Christ our Lord:

> *Remember also those who have died in the peace of your Christ and all the dead, whose faith you alone have known.*
>
> *To all of us, your children, grant, O merciful Father, that we may enter into a heavenly inheritance with the Blessed Virgin Mary, Mother of God, with blessed Joseph, her Spouse, and with your Apostles and Saints in your kingdom.*
>
> *There, with the whole of creation, freed from the corruption of sin and death, may we glorify you through Christ our Lord, through whom you bestow on the world all that is good.*

As in Eucharistic Prayers I and III, after acknowledging that all blessings on the world come from God through Jesus, the celebrant then concludes Eucharistic Prayer IV with the usual proclamation that all glory from earth goes to God through Jesus.

And so, it is my earnest hope that the careful reflections we have made on the wording of the four ordinary Eucharistic Prayers will deeply enrich our understanding of the Mass. As a result, may we enter more consciously and sincerely into the total offering of ourselves and our lives to God, in union with the Self-Offering of Jesus to His Father in total love and obedience. Miraculously and marvelously the eternal moment of His redeeming Self-Offering on Calvary is made present to us by the Consecration of the bread and wine into His Body and Blood during the Holy Sacrifice of the Mass. Therefore, let us surrender ourselves to God *At Mass with Jesus on Calvary*!

Endnote for Chapter 4

[1] Here is a brief reflection on these four words:

The word <u>gift</u> refers to something that is given from one person to another without the giver expecting any kind of compensation. We associate this word especially with occasions like birthday parties or Christmas time; (gifts received on such occasions are also called "presents"). Usually the giving of gifts implies friendship or love between the parties involved. The Eucharistic Prayers speak both of our gifts to God and God's gifts to us.

The word <u>offering</u> may refer to a donation of some kind. However, unlike the word <u>gift</u>, it is more readily associated with an act of worship or devotion. In the Eucharistic Prayers <u>offering</u>, as you would expect, refers to something which we offer to God in association with the bread and wine on the altar. Outside the Eucharistic Prayers, the word <u>offering</u> sometimes refers to the money we put into the collection basket.

The word <u>oblation</u> is more closely associated with religious worship than either of the previous two words. Perhaps this is because it comes from the Latin word *oblatus,* which means "something that is offered." In *Webster's Seventh New Collegiate Dictionary,* one definition of this word is, "a religious offering of something inanimate." Another is, "something offered in worship." Even more directly associated with the celebration of Mass, the dictionary defines Oblation (i.e. <u>oblation </u>written with a Capital "O") as the "Act of offering the Eucharistic elements to God."

Finally, the word <u>sacrifice,</u> which has meanings in no way associated with worship—such as "a sacrifice bunt" in the game of baseball, or "the sacrifices which parents make for their children"— always implies the enduring of some hardship on the part of the one making the sacrifice. The word <u>sacrifice</u> is more closely associated with the worship of a deity than any of the other three words above. It can refer both to the act of offering and to what is offered, especially when the offering is an animal which is slain during the act of being offered to the deity. In the Eucharistic Prayers <u>sacrifice</u> refers primarily to the death of Jesus.

15th Century Roman Missal, courtesy of Wikimedia, https://commons.wikimedia.org/wiki/File:Roman_missal_(15th_c entury).jpg

CHAPTER FIVE

THE BIBLE IN THE MASS

The Words of Scripture
in the Ordinary Prayers of the Mass

In the practice of our Catholic Faith, there is an obvious difference between reading the Bible and assisting at Mass. Also, recent generations of Catholics seem to engage much more than did former generations of good Catholics, in the reading and study of the Bible itself, as a separate activity. But I wonder whether most Catholics realize how much of the Bible is actually to be found in the Mass itself. Whether or not Catholics read the Bible outside of the Mass, they hear many passages from the Bible every time they attend Mass.

In every weekday celebration of the Mass two extended passages from Scripture are read aloud to the congregation—and on Sundays three. In addition, at least part of one of the Psalms in the Bible is always read aloud at Mass.

Perhaps some Catholics do not realize that they hear the Bible read to them so often because it is read, not directly from a copy of the Bible itself, but out of a "Lectionary," that is, a collection of Bible Readings prepared specifically for use in the celebration of the Mass. These readings are adapted to the spirit of the liturgical seasons and to the feast days of individual Saints. Moreover, in addition to these longer passages from the

Bible that are read during the Mass, almost every prayer in what are called the "Ordinary Prayers of the Mass"[1] is based upon some passage found in Sacred Scripture; often enough the prayer is either a direct quotation or a paraphrase of the Scripture passage itself.

In this chapter, let us look at some of these Scripture passages as they relate to the prayers of the Mass. I will not try to give references to all the Scripture passages that may be related to a particular prayer. In some instances, I will merely quote the prayer from the Mass and then the passage from Scripture. Thus the reader can easily compare them. At other times I will comment further on the meaning of the prayer or Scripture passage. Sometimes I will underline, or print in bold, parts of a prayer or a Scripture passage, in order to help clarify their relationship to each other. Let us begin at the beginning of the Mass.

THE SIGN OF THE CROSS

Prayer of the Mass: *In the name of the Father and of the Son and of the Holy Spirit*

Scripture: Mt. 28, 18-19: Jesus came forward and addressed them in these words: ... "Baptize them in the name of the Father, and of the Son, and of the Holy Spirit...."

The Sign of the Cross is made by Catholics at the beginning and end of most prayers. Using the words of Jesus himself, we proclaim that we live our lives in light of our Baptism, united with the God –Father, Son, and Holy Spirit –who has given us our life on this earth. It should be prayed thoughtfully as a kind of "mini" Profession of Faith.

AMEN

To the "Sign of the Cross" which opens every celebration of the Eucharist, and to most (but not all) of the prayers throughout the Mass which are prayed by the celebrant, the congregation answers with the word "Amen." In fact, most of the prayers Catholics pray at any time end with the word "Amen." Moreover, we are so used to the word <u>amen</u>, which has become a common response to another person's words in situations which have nothing to do with the Mass, that it may surprise us that "Amen" is actually a word taken from Scripture. It is used at least a dozen times in both the Old and New Testaments. In some translations of the Gospels, Jesus uses it repeatedly to draw attention to what he is saying. In the Book of Revelation, Jesus is actually referred to as the "Amen."

The word <u>amen</u> is found, in fact, in many languages. It means "true," "faithful," "certain," or "so be it." It is used to give emphasis or confirmation to something which is said. I will give only a few examples from Scripture.

Prayer of the Mass: *Amen.*

Scripture: Jeremiah 28, 5-6: The prophet Jeremiah answered the prophet Hananiah in the presence of the priests and all the people assembled in the house of the Lord, and said: "Amen! Thus may the Lord do!"

Psalm 72, 19: And blessed forever be his glorious name; may the whole earth be filled with his glory. Amen. Amen.

John 10, 1 (Confraternity[2] translation)**:** Amen, amen, I say to you, he who enters not by the door into the sheepfold, but climbs up another way, is a thief and a robber. (The New American Bible reads: "Truly I assure you," etc.)

Revelation 3, 14: To the presiding spirit of the church in Laodicea, write this: "The Amen, the faithful Witness and true, the Source of God's creation has this to say...."

OPENING GREETING

After the Sign of the Cross, the celebrant addresses the congregation with one of the following greetings:

Prayer of the Mass: *The grace of our Lord Jesus Christ, and the love of God, and the communion of the Holy Spirit be with you all.*

Scripture: St. Paul ends his second Letter to the Corinthians, with the words: "The grace of the Lord Jesus Christ, and the love of God, and the fellowship of the Holy Spirit be with you all!" **(2 Cor. 13, 13)**

Or:

Prayer of the Mass: *Grace to you and peace from God our Father and the Lord Jesus Christ.*

Scripture: These are almost the exact words which St. Paul uses at the beginning of many of his letters:

Romans 1, 7:...To all in Rome, beloved of God and called to holiness, grace and peace from God our Father and the Lord Jesus Christ.

1 Corinthians 1, 3: Grace and peace from God our Father and the Lord Jesus Christ.

2 Corinthians 1, 2: Grace and peace from God our Father

and the Lord Jesus Christ.

Galatians 1, 3: We wish you the favor and peace of God our Father and of the Lord Jesus Christ.

Ephesians 1, 2: Grace and peace to you from God our Father and the Lord Jesus Christ.

Philippians 1, 2: Grace and peace be yours from God our Father and from the Lord Jesus Christ.

2 Thessalonians 1, 2: Grace and peace from God our Father and the Lord Jesus Christ.

Titus 1, 4: May grace and peace from God our Father and Christ Jesus our Savior be with you.

Philemon 1, 3: Grace to you and peace from God our Father and from the Lord Jesus Christ.

Or:

Prayer of the Mass: *The Lord be with you.*

Scripture: The Book of Ruth 2, 4: Boaz himself came from Bethlehem and said to the harvesters, "The Lord be with you!"

1 Chronicles 22, 11: Now, my son, the Lord be with you and may you succeed....

1 Chronicles 22, 16: Set to work, therefore, and the Lord be with you!

PENITENTIAL RITE

During the penitential rite the celebrant prays over the congregation,

Prayer of the Mass: *May almighty God have mercy on us, forgive us our sins, and bring us to everlasting life.*

Scripture: With its reference to God's mercy, the celebrant's prayer seems to reflect the spirit of the following passages:

Letter of Jude 1, 2: May mercy, peace, and love be yours in ever greater measure.

1 Timothy 1, 2: May grace, mercy, and peace be yours from God the Father and from Christ Jesus our Lord.

2 Timothy 1, 2: May grace mercy and peace from God the Father and from Christ Jesus our Lord be with you.

2 John 1, 3: In truth and love, then we shall have grace, mercy and peace from God the Father and from Jesus Christ, Son of the Father.

Matt. 17, 15: Lord, take pity on my son.

GLORIA

Prayer of the Mass: *Glory to God in the highest, and on earth peace to people of good will. We praise you, we bless you, we adore you, we glorify you, we give you thanks for your great glory, Lord God, heavenly King, O God, almighty Father. Lord Jesus Christ, Only Begotten* Son,*

Lord God, Lamb of God, Son of the Father, you take away the sins of the world, have mercy on us; you take away the sins of the world, receive our prayer; you are seated at the right hand of the Father, have mercy on us. For you alone are the Holy One, you alone are the Lord, you alone are the Most High, Jesus Christ, with the Holy Spirit, in the glory of God the Father. Amen

The Gloria of the Mass is a prayer of praise to God the Father and to Jesus, the Incarnate Son of the Father, in union with the Holy Spirit, who is mentioned towards the end of the prayer. Its composition utilizes or reflects many passages from Scripture. I will repeat the words of the Gloria section by section to show more easily its relation to Scripture.

Prayer of the Mass: *Glory to God in the highest, and on earth peace to people of good will.*

Scripture: Lk. 2, 13-14: Suddenly there was with the angel a multitude of the heavenly host, praising God and saying, 'Glory to God in high heaven, peace on earth to those on whom his favor rests.'

Prayer of the Mass: *We praise you, we bless you, we adore you, we glorify you, we give you thanks for your great glory, Lord God, heavenly King, O God, almighty Father.*

Scripture: Psalm 66, 4: Let all on earth worship and <u>sing praise</u> to you, sing praise to your name"

Psalm 105, 2-3: Sing to him, <u>sing his praise</u>, proclaim all his wondrous deeds. <u>Glory in his holy name</u>; rejoice hearts that seek the Lord!

Eph. 1, 11-12, 17: ...we were predestined <u>to praise his glory</u>; ....May the God of our Lord Jesus Christ, <u>the Father of glory</u>....

Prayer of the Mass: *Lord Jesus Christ, Only Begotten* Son, Lord God, Lamb of God, Son of the Father, you take away the sins of the world, have mercy on us; you take away the sins of the world, receive our prayer; you are seated at the right hand of the Father, have mercy on us.*

Scripture: 1 John 4, 9: ...he sent <u>his only Son</u> to the world

John 1, 29: The next day, when John caught sight of Jesus coming toward him, he explained: "Look! there is the <u>Lamb of God who takes away the sin of the world!</u>"

Mk. 16, 19: Then, after speaking to them, the Lord Jesus was taken up into heaven and <u>took his seat at God's right hand</u>.

Heb. 1, 3: When he had cleansed us of our sins, <u>he took his seat at the right hand of the Majesty in heaven</u>....

The following words express titles of Divinity given to Jesus:

Prayer of the Mass: *For you alone are the **Holy One**, you alone are the **Lord**, you alone are the **Most High**,*

Scripture: Acts 2, 36: Therefore let the whole house of Israel know beyond any doubt that God has made both <u>Lord</u> and Messiah this Jesus whom you crucified.

Exodus 33, 19: Then Moses said, "Do let me see your glory!" He answered, "I will make all my beauty pass before

you, and in your presence I will pronounce my name, 'Lord'"
Exodus 34, 5-6: Having come down in a cloud, the Lord
stood with him there and proclaimed his name, Lord."
Thus the Lord passed before him and cried out, "The Lord,
the Lord, a merciful and gracious God, slow to anger and rich
in kindness and fidelity...."

Isaiah 10, 20: But they will lean upon the Lord, the Holy
One of Israel, in truth.

Numbers 24, 16: The utterance of one who hears what
God says, and knows what the Most High knows...

Prayer of the Mass: *Jesus Christ, with the Holy Spirit, in
the glory of God the Father.*

Scripture: Acts 7, 55: Stephen meanwhile, filled with the
Holy Spirit, looked to the sky above and saw the glory of God
and Jesus standing at God's right hand. "Look!" he exclaimed, "I see an opening in the sky, and the Son of Man
standing at God's right hand."

In these final words of the "Gloria," in which Jesus, along
with the Holy Spirit, is once more acclaimed as sharing the glory
of God the Father, we see a brief expression of the Doctrine of
the Blessed Trinity.

ALLELUIA

The Alleluia of the Mass is that short prayer which is sung
just before the reading of the Gospel. Actually, it is one of the
Proper Prayers of the Mass rather than one of the Ordinary
Prayers. But its relationship to Scripture merits mention here.
It is intended to be a cry of joyful praise to God in anticipation

of the reading from one of the New Testament Gospels which we are about to hear. The word "alleluia" is sung before and after a verse which is usually a few words taken from the coming Gospel. The word "Alleluia" is always the same, but the verse which accompanies it changes according to the Proper Prayers for any given Mass text.

The word alleluia itself, which also appears in the form Hallelujah, is a Hebrew word which means "Praise Yahweh." It appears at the beginning or the end, or both the beginning and the end of about sixteen psalms;[3] I will quote only one of these psalms. Alleluia also appears and is repeated a few times in the first several verses of chapter 19 of the Book of Revelation.

Prayer of the Mass: *Alleluia!*

Scripture: Psalm 136: Alleluia. Give thanks to the Lord for he is good, for his mercy endures forever, etc....

Revelation 19, 1-6: After this I heard what sounded like the loud song of a great assembly in heaven. They were singing: "Alleluia! Salvation, glory and might belong to our God, for his judgments are true and just....Once more they sang, "Alleluia!"...the four and twenty elders and the four living creatures fell down and worshiped God seated on the throne and sang, "Amen! Alleluia!"...then I heard what sounded like the shouts of a great crowd...as they cried, "Alleluia! The Lord is king, our God the Almighty!"

THE PROFESSION OF FAITH

At all Masses on Sundays and Solemn Feast Days, after the reading of the Gospel and the homily which usually follows, the Profession of Faith is recited by the celebrant and congregation together, just before the Prayer of the Faithful and the preparation of gifts. The Profession of Faith is what its title says it is—not simply a prayer prayed together—but rather a solemn proclamation or "Profession" of the truths of our Catholic Faith. Standing side by side all together as a community, each of us tells one another and the world at large what it is that Catholics believe.

In reflecting on the Profession of Faith, our approach will be somewhat different and more prolonged than it has been with the other Ordinary Prayers of the Mass which have preceded it or will come after it. There is not so much a need to identify individual passages of Scripture which are reflected in this prayer of the Mass, but there is a need to explain its rather complicated structure and meaning. Before reflecting on the actual wording of the Profession of Faith itself, however, it will be helpful to reflect on Jesus himself.

On Christmas every year we celebrate the birth of Jesus. As we know, his mother, Mary, gave birth to him a little over 2000 years ago. For nine months before his birth, having been conceived through the miraculous power of the Holy Spirit, Jesus was a developing embryo in his mother's womb, just like all human babies. But prior to the moment of his conception in Mary's womb, Jesus did not exist. For those many millennia of human history on earth, from the beginning of the human race until approximately 4 B.C. there was no Jesus, Son of God. Jesus began to exist only a little over 2000 years ago, when his mother conceived and afterwards gave birth to him. Before that time, i.e. approximately 4 B.C., hundreds of generations of human beings existed; the Chosen People of God existed; Abraham, Moses, David, and the Prophets existed; but Jesus did not exist.[4]

However, the Only Begotten* Son of the Father did exist, God from all eternity, together with the Father and the Holy Spirit. And so, the Only Begotten Son of the Father—but not Jesus—existed not only during all the millennia of human history, but during the total evolution of the universe, and, from all eternity, even before the beginning of creation itself.

What took place at the very moment that Mary conceived Jesus as an embryo in her womb about 2000 years ago, was that the Only Begotten Son of the Father united Himself with Jesus in so close a union, that Mary's new child existed not only in his own human nature—like all human babies conceived by their mothers—but also in union with the divine nature of the Father's Only Begotten Son. However, there were not now two Sons of the Father, but still only the one Divine Person of the Blessed Trinity, with the newly existing human nature of Jesus joined intimately to his divine nature.

We cannot figure out—nor should we try to do so —how God brought about this miraculous union. But as Catholics we firmly believe that God did bring it about; and in reflecting upon this deep mystery of our Faith, theologians have called it the *Hypostatic Union,* which means a union in the Person. The Council of Ephesus, in 431, speaks of it this way: "...by uniting to himself in his own person a body animated by a rational soul, the Word has become man in an inexpressible and incomprehensible way....both divinity and humanity produce the perfection of our one Lord, Christ and Son, by their inexpressible and mysterious joining into unity...."5 And because of this union the newly conceived Jesus is truthfully called, not a second Son of God, but rather the Only Begotten Son of the Father, even though the human Jesus was not conceived and born until long after the beginning of time and the eternal existence of God the Son Himself. And so, before he was conceived by Mary, there was no Jesus to be called the Only Begotten* Son of God; but, from the first moment of his existence in Mary's womb, he is truly the Only Begotten* Son of God.

In the early centuries of the Church's history after Jesus ascended into heaven, the beliefs of Christians about Jesus came to be formally expressed in what we know as The Apostles Creed.

The Apostles Creed, while probably not written by the Apostles themselves, dates from at least the late fourth century. It summarizes the teachings of the Church from its earliest days. Most Catholics are familiar with it as the prayer prayed at the beginning of the recitation of the Rosary. It is also used at times as the "Profession of Faith" during the Mass. It professes belief in God (Father, Son, and Holy Spirit) as Creator of heaven and earth. It proclaims the Incarnation of God's Only Begotten Son in Jesus Christ, including his conception, his birth, life, death, resurrection, ascension into heaven, and his coming at the end of time to judge the living and the dead. It also expresses belief in one holy, catholic and apostolic Church, the forgiveness of sins, the communion of saints,[6] the resurrection the body, and life everlasting. We will reflect on most of these truths as we study the wording of the Profession of Faith.

In the early centuries of Christianity, however, despite The Apostles Creed, there arose teachers in the Church who denied the divinity or the full humanity of Jesus, as well as the divinity of the Holy Spirit. To counteract these heresies the Church's Bishops—beginning early during the fourth century—gathered repeatedly in Ecumenical Councils to proclaim the true teaching of the Church about Jesus. The phrases of our Profession of Faith, in which we spell out clearly and emphatically what we believe about Jesus, are closely based upon the declarations of these Councils. The first was the Council of Nicaea, held in 325A.D. Next was the Council of Constantinople, in 381A.D. Then came the Council of Ephesus, in 431A.D. and the Council of Chalcedon, in 451A.D. Not long after this latter council, what is known as the Niceno-Constantinopolitan Creed appeared in the liturgy of the Eastern Church; and by the year 800AD it was also introduced into the liturgy of the Western Church. Finally, about eight centuries later, in 1564, the Council of Trent issued its Profession of Faith, which differed very little from the declaration of the Council of Nicaea more than a thousand years earlier. Today, still another five centuries after Trent, the present Latin version of the Profession of Faith (on which our English translation is based) is identical with the 1564 declaration of the Council of Trent.[7]

So let us now reflect carefully on the complete wording of the Profession of Faith, which reasserts and amplifies the teachings of the Apostles Creed. What we profess individually, but also as a community joined together in the celebration of the Eucharist, are the same beliefs which Catholic Christians have always believed from the time of the Apostles onwards.

In order to make our reflections easier to understand, I will first display the Profession of Faith in its entirety and then break it down into individual sections.

I believe in one God, the Father almighty, maker of heaven and earth, of all things visible and invisible. I believe in one Lord Jesus Christ, the Only Begotten* Son of God, born of the Father before all ages. God from God, Light from Light, true God from true God, begotten, not made, consubstantial with the Father; through him all things were made. For us men and for our salvation he came down from heaven, and by the Holy Spirit was incarnate of the Virgin Mary, and became man. For our sake he was crucified under Pontius Pilate, he suffered death and was buried, and rose again on the third day in accordance with the Scriptures. He ascended into heaven and is seated at the right hand of the Father. He will come again in glory to judge the living and the dead and his kingdom will have no end. I believe in the Holy Spirit, the Lord, the giver of life, who proceeds from the Father and the Son, who with the Father and the Son is adored and glorified, who has spoken through the prophets. I believe in one, holy, catholic and apostolic Church. I confess one Baptism for the forgiveness of sins and I look forward to the resurrection of the dead and the life of the *world to come. Amen.*

In order to help us understand some of the phrases in the wording of the Profession of Faith, it will be necessary to join them together in a somewhat different word-order from that given above. This re-arrangement of words does not change the meaning of the Profession of Faith, but it helps to make that meaning clear. We begin with God the Father and creation:

I believe in one God, the Father almighty, maker of heaven and earth, of all things visible and invisible.

We believe that we and the universe we live in do not exist of ourselves. We cannot take credit for our own being, for who we are. We have a meaning and purpose beyond our earthly existence. We believe that there is a God who has created us in time along with all other creatures, many of whom we do not see, such as the angels. We believe that God is infinite in being, power, goodness, beauty, knowledge, and love. And so we say He is "almighty." In his divine nature, God is Father, Only Begotten Son, and Holy Spirit. But He is also our Father, and we consider ourselves his children.

Next we express what we believe about Jesus of Nazareth.

I believe in one Lord Jesus Christ

As we have seen above, what we believe about Jesus is complex. In his human existence, he did not appear in the generations of human beings on earth until about

4 BC. But we call him "Lord" because we believe that he is not merely human, but also Divine. This doctrine of our Faith is expressed in a number of places in the New Testament, among them in various letters of St. Paul.

For example, in his Letter to the Philippians Paul writes, "So that at Jesus' name every knee must bend in the heavens, on the earth, and under the earth, and every tongue proclaim to the glory of God the Father: JESUS CHRIST IS LORD!" **(Phil. 2, 10-11)** As we saw in reflecting on the Gloria of the Mass, "Lord" was a title indicating Divinity.

> *the Only Begotten* Son of God...born of the Father before all ages.. .begotten,* not made, consubstantial with the Father.*

These words indicate first of all that Jesus, in his Divine nature, is generated, or "begotten" by God the Father, not in the sense that the Father came first and afterwards gave birth to the Son. No, the Son was not "made" by the Father. Rather, from all eternity the One God's nature is three-fold: the Father begetting the Son, and the Holy Spirit proceeding from both Father and Son, in one, simple, yet three-fold love relationship. All three Persons of the Blessed Trinity are equally God and exist simultaneously without beginning or end in their relationship with one another, which is The Divine Love Reality which we call "God." God's Nature is To Be. And so, in Nature and Being God is simple, not complex. God is one. As we saw in Chapter One of this book, *"Substance"* is what makes something be what it is. What makes the Father to be God is the same substance which also makes the Son to be God and the Holy Spirit to be God. This is what is meant by saying that the Son is "consubstantial" with the Father (and so is the Holy Spirit). That is, the Son has the same substance as the Father, the same Nature and Being. And the full truth of this reality is emphasized, further elaborated, and applied to Jesus as the Incarnate Word, by the following phrases,

> *God from God, Light from Light, true God from true God.*
Jesus, then, because of his Hypostatic Union with the Only

Begotten Son of the Father is "God from God." God is often referred to in Scripture as "Light"; and so Jesus is said also to be Light from Light. St. John expresses this early in his Gospel **(John 1, 9)**, when he writes that, "The true light that enlightens every man was coming into the world." Again, in **John 8, 12**, Jesus himself says, "I am the light of the world." Finally, Jesus is called "True God from true God," again because of his Hypostatic union with God the Son.

Next we have the words,

through him all things were made.

Because of his consubstantial union with God the Father, who is "the Creator of all things, visible and invisible," it is truly said that all things are created through his Only Begotten Son. Because of the Hypostatic Union, it is also truly said that all things were created through Jesus. Both St. John and St. Paul, attribute this characteristic to Jesus:

John 1, 3: "Through him all things came into being, and apart from him nothing came to be."

Colossians 1, 15-16: "He is the image of the invisible God, the first-born of all creatures. In him everything in heaven and on earth was created, things visible and invisible..."

Next we profess our belief in the actual Incarnation of the Father's Only Begotten Son, which came about through Mary's conceiving and giving birth to Jesus.

For us men and for our salvation he came down from heaven, and by the Holy Spirit was incarnate of the Virgin Mary, and became man.

First of all, God willed the Incarnation for the sake of the human race, in order to save us from sin and death and bring us to eternal happiness in heaven. But when we say that "he came down from heaven" we must not misunderstand the meaning of these words. They do not express a geographical movement. Rather, they refer to the beginning, here on earth, of the Hypostatic Union which took place the moment Mary conceived Jesus about 2000 years ago. As God, being consubstantial with the Father, the Only Begotten Son is from all eternity and always has been everywhere, both in heaven and on earth. He does not need to leave one place to be in another. Remember, again, that before his conception by his mother Mary about the year 4B.C. Jesus did not exist. Therefore, Jesus had not been in heaven waiting to come down on earth. Jesus began on earth. The "coming down from heaven," then, refers to the unique Hypostatic Union of the Only Begotten Son of the Father with Jesus when he began his existence in his mother's womb.

Let us remind ourselves, too, that we are dealing here with a supernatural mystery which our natural reason cannot fully understand and which we can know only by Faith. While the Only Begotten Son of God is unchangeable, still, in our human experience his incarnation in Jesus is for us a new and tangible expression of his presence on earth. Perhaps it will be helpful to apply to the Incarnation those words used by the Council of Trent in speaking of the Eucharist: "We can hardly find words to express this way of existing; but our reason, guided by faith, can know that it is possible for God, and this we should always believe unhesitatingly."

Finally, the words "by the Holy Spirit (he) was incarnate of the Virgin Mary, and became man" express our belief in the manner in which the Incarnation, with its Hypostatic Union, took place through Mary's conception of Jesus. Again, "became man" does not mean that the Divine Only Begotten Son was changed into a human being but rather that the Hypostatic

Union of the Only Begotten Son and Jesus did indeed take place at the first moment of his existence, uniting Jesus the man, in his human nature, with God the Son, the Divine Second Person of the Blessed Trinity.

> *For our sake he was crucified under Pontius Pilate, he suffered death and was buried, and rose again on the third day in accordance with the Scriptures. He ascended into heaven and is seated at the right hand of the Father. He will come again in glory to judge the living and the dead and his kingdom will have no end.*

In the above words, we say that we believe that Jesus died by crucifixion through the order of the Roman procurator Pontius Pilate, but that he rose from death three days later, as prophesied in the Old Testament.[8] Furthermore, we believe that he ascended bodily into heaven, where, in what is now his natural way of existing, he is always at the right hand of the Father (interceding for us); but we also believe that at the end of time he will appear again on earth to judge all human beings of all times, those who have already died and those who are still living at the time of his second coming. Finally, we declare that the kingdom of Jesus, begun on earth, will continue forever in heaven.

Next we profess our belief in the Holy Spirit.

> *I believe in the Holy Spirit, the Lord, the giver of life, who proceeds from the Father and the Son, who with the Father and the Son is adored and glorified, who has spoken through the prophets.*

As I mentioned earlier, the divinity of the Holy Spirit was denied by some teachers in the early Church but affirmed, along with the divinity of Jesus, by the Ecumenical Councils. The teaching of the Church is that, in a Trinity of Love from all eternity, without beginning or end, the Holy Spirit is simultaneously present with the Father and the Son, as the "personalized reality" of their love for each other; and because the Holy Spirit is the Mutual Love of the Father and the Son, He is said "to proceed from the Father and the Son." And so, we believe that, like the Son, the Holy Spirit is also Lord and consubstantial with the Father. Therefore we adore him along with the Father and the Son and acknowledge his role in inspiring the prophets and in dwelling within us as God's Life.

I believe in one, holy, catholic* and apostolic Church.

Here we express our belief in the catholic Church, established by Jesus—before he ascended into heaven—to continue and spread throughout the world the teaching and practice which He had begun during his short time (33 years) living on earth.[9]

This Church is <u>one</u>, united in its doctrine and worship throughout the world.

This Church is <u>holy</u>. Despite the sinfulness of its members, the Church, through the Sacraments, sanctifies them and enables them to live good lives on earth, in union with the All-Holy God. The holiness of the Church is especially seen in the lives of its many canonized Saints.

This Church is <u>catholic</u>.* Here the word is used, not in its usual sense with a capital "C," which distinguishes the Catholic Church from Protestant Christians and other non-Catholic religions in the world; but, more importantly, in the sense that it is universal. It is God's chosen means to bring <u>all human beings in the world</u> to eternal salvation through Jesus Christ.[10]

This Church is <u>apostolic</u> because it traces its existence back through the centuries to the Apostles of Jesus themselves as they carried out Jesus' commission to bring his Gospel to the whole world and to baptize all persons "in the name of the Father and of the Son, and of the Holy Spirit."

I confess* one Baptism for the forgiveness of sins and I look forward to the resurrection of the dead and the life of the world to come. Amen.

Finally, in the above words, we express our belief in the Baptism commanded by Jesus, which is given to each individual once and for all, to save us from sin; and we proclaim belief in the resurrection of our bodies at the end of time and a life of unending happiness with God.

We have now completed our lengthy reflections on the theologically complex, but profoundly meaningful, Profession of Faith as it appears among the Ordinary Prayers of the Mass.

PREPARATION OF THE GIFTS

Prayer of the Mass: *Blessed are you,* **Lord God of all creation***, for through your goodness* **we have received the bread** *we offer you, etc.*

Prayer of the Mass: *Blessed are you Lord God of all creation, for through your goodness* **we have received the wine** *we offer you, etc.*

Scripture: Psalm 115, 15: May you be blessed by the Lord, **who made heaven and earth**

Acts 14, 15: We are bringing you the good news that will convert you from just such follies as these to **the living God, 'the one who made heaven and earth and the**

sea and all that is in them.'

Psalm 104, 14-15: You raise grass for the cattle, and vegetation for men's use, **producing bread from the earth, and wine to gladden men's hearts.**

Psalm 116, 13: The cup of salvation I will take up, and I will call upon the name of the Lord.

This verse of Psalm 116 expresses the celebrant's actions, rather than his words, as he offers the bread and the wine at this moment of the Mass; and so it shows how even some of the actions of the Mass, as well as its prayers, are based on the words of Scripture.

HOLY, HOLY, HOLY

Prayer of the Mass: *Holy, holy, holy Lord God of hosts. Heaven and earth are full of your glory. Hosanna in the highest. Blessed is he who comes in the name of the Lord. Hosanna in the highest.*

Scripture: Isaiah 6, 3: "Holy, holy, holy is the Lord of hosts!" they cried one to the other. "All the earth is filled with his glory!"

Mt. 21, 9: The groups preceding him as well as those following kept crying out: "Hosanna to the Son of David! Blessed is he who comes in the name of the Lord! Hosanna in the highest!"

Psalm 118, 26: Blessed is he who comes in the name of the Lord.

OUR FATHER

The "Our Father" is perhaps the most well-known of all Catholic prayers. It is prayed not only during the Mass but also at the beginning of each decade of the Rosary. This prayer was given to us by Jesus himself, as we read in the Gospels of Matthew and Luke. The petitions which are expressed in the "Our Father" are reminiscent of many other passages in Scripture, especially in the Psalms. I will print the prayer as a whole, and afterwards I will print individual petitions to illustrate some of these similarities.

Prayer of the Mass: *Our Father, who art in heaven, hallowed be thy name; thy kingdom come, thy will be done on earth as it is in heaven. Give us this day our daily bread, and forgive us our trespasses, as we forgive those who trespass against us; and lead us not into temptation, but deliver us from evil.*

Scripture: Mt. 6, 9-13: This is how you are to pray: Our Father in heaven, hallowed be your name, your kingdom come, your will be done on earth as it is in heaven. Give us today our daily bread, and forgive us the wrong we have done as we forgive those who wrong us. Subject us not to the trial but deliver us from the evil one.

Luke 11, 2-4: He said to them, "When you pray, say: Father, hallowed be your name, your kingdom come. Give us each day our daily bread. Forgive us our sins for we too forgive all who do us wrong; and subject us not to the trial."

Our Father

Psalm 89, 27: "He shall say of me, 'You are my father, my

God the rock, my savior.'"

Hallowed be thy name

Psalm 29, 2: Give to the Lord the glory due his name....

Thy kingdom come

Psalm 145, 11&12: Let them discourse of the glory of your kingdom and speak of your might, making known to men your might and the glorious splendor of your kingdom. Your kingdom is a kingdom for all ages, and your dominion endures through all generations.

Thy will be done on earth as it is in heaven

Psalm 135, 6: All that the Lord wills he does in heaven and on earth....

Give us this day our daily bread

Psalm 132, 15: I will bless her with abundant provision, her poor I will fill with bread

Forgive us our trespasses as we forgive those who trespass against us

Luke 6, 37: Pardon, and you shall be pardoned.

Mark 11, 25: When you stand to pray, forgive anyone against whom you have a grievance so that your heavenly Father may in turn forgive you your faults.

And lead us not into temptation, but deliver us from evil

Psalm 19, 13: Yet who can detect failings? Cleanse me of my unknown faults.

Psalm 121, 7: The Lord will guard you from all evil; he will guard your life.

DELIVER US LORD

This prayer of the celebrant begins as an extension of the final petition of the "Our Father" ("deliver us from evil") and is actually concluded with the response of the congregation.

Prayer of the Mass: *Deliver us, Lord, we pray, from every evil, graciously grant peace in our days, that, by the help of your mercy, we may be always free from sin and safe from all distress,* **as we await the blessed hope and the coming** *of our Savior, Jesus Christ.*

Scripture: 1 Cor. 1, 6-7: Likewise, the witness I bore to Christ has been so confirmed among you that you lack no spiritual gift as you **wait for the revelation** of our Lord Jesus Christ.

1 Cor. 15, 22-23: Just as in Adam all die, so in Christ all will come to life again, but each one in proper order: Christ the first fruits and then, **at his coming,** all those who belong to him.

1 Thess. 2, 19: Who, after all, if not you, will be our hope or joy, or the crown we exult in, before our Lord Jesus Christ **at his coming?**

Titus 2, 13: ...as we await our blessed hope, the ap-

pearing of the glory of the Great God and our Savior Christ Jesus

Prayer of the Mass: *For the kingdom, the power, and the glory are yours now and forever.*

Scripture: 1 Chr. 29, 11: Yours, O Lord, are grandeur and power, majesty, splendor, and glory, for all in heaven and on earth is yours; **yours, O Lord, is the sovereignty**; you are exalted as head over all.

Psalm 22, 29: For **dominion is the Lord's** and he rules the nations

Obadiah, 21: ...and the kingship shall be the Lord's.

Mt. 6, 9-10: This is how you are to pray: 'Our Father in heaven, hallowed be your name, **your kingdom come....**'

SIGN OF PEACE PRAYER

Prayer of the Mass: *Lord Jesus Christ, who said to your Apostles: **Peace I leave you, my peace I give you;** look not on our sins, but on the faith of your Church, and graciously grant her **peace and unity** in accordance with your will.*

Scripture: John 14, 27: 'Peace' is my **farewell** to you, **my peace is my gift to you....**"

John 16, 33: I tell you all this that **in me you may find peace**

1 Cor. 10, 17: Because the loaf of bread is **one**, we, many though we are, are **one** body, for we all partake of the **one** loaf.

LAMB OF GOD

In the prayer, "Lamb of God" we see clearly the words of St. John the Baptist to Jesus' first apostles.

Prayer of the Mass: *Lamb of God, you take away the sins of the world, have mercy on us. Lamb of God, you take away the sins of the world, have mercy on us. Lamb of God, you take away the sins of the world, grant us peace.*

Scripture: John 1, 29: The next day, when John caught sight of Jesus coming toward him, he exclaimed: "Look! There is the **Lamb of God who takes away the sin of the world!**"

COMMUNION

Prayer of the Mass: *Lord, I am not worthy that you should enter under my roof, but only say the word and my soul shall be healed.*

Scripture: Luke 7, 2 & 6-7: A centurion had a servant he held in high regard, who was at that moment sick to the point of death.... Jesus set out with them. When he was only a short distance from the house, the centurion sent friends to tell him" "Sir, do not trouble yourself, for **I am not worthy to have you enter my house.... Just give the order and my servant will be cured.**"

This prayer of the congregation just before the distribution of Holy Communion in the Mass is clearly based upon the above words of the centurion, in St. Luke's Gospel, who had sent word to Jesus asking him to come and heal his servant. In our prayer before Communion, of course, we substitute the word "soul" for "servant." And when we pray "under my roof" we are referring not to our houses, but to Jesus' coming into our whole person through our bodies.

This completes our reflections on the close relationship between the Ordinary Prayers of the Mass and the Bible. As we have seen, at times the Prayers of the Mass are identical with the words of Scripture, at other times they are a paraphrase. At still other times they vividly reflect the underlying thought of a particular Scripture passage.

And so we come to realize that the Words of Scripture themselves are an intimate, all-pervasive, and essential component of every celebration of the Mass. For whenever the Mass is celebrated, Jesus comes to be with us both through these words of Holy Scripture and in the miracle of His Eucharistic Presence.

This concludes our reflections upon the Holy Sacrifice of the Mass itself. Our final chapter will deal with other reflections associated with the Eucharist outside of the actual celebration of the Mass.

Endnotes for Chapter 5

[1] Perhaps a fuller explanation of the Liturgy of the Church would be helpful at this time. By "liturgy" we mean the various religious celebrations or services which take place in the Church, especially the celebration of the Mass. The year-long period during which these celebrations take place is called "The Liturgical Year," which begins with the First Sunday of Advent, near the end of November or the beginning of December, and ends with the 34th Week in "Ordinary Time," which immediately precedes the First Sunday of Advent.

The Liturgical Year is divided into several seasons: Advent Season, Christmas Season, Lenten Season, Easter Triduum, Easter Season, and Ordinary Time, which is scattered among the other liturgical seasons. There are particular prayers and readings from Scripture for each season, as well as for Masses in honor of the Saints, special feasts in honor of Jesus or the Blessed Trinity, and for other liturgical celebrations, such as marriages, funerals, civic holidays, etc.

The priest who celebrates the Mass consults a small-calendar book which is called the "Ordo" in order to see what Mass texts are prescribed for any particular day of the year. Some seasonal celebrations or feast days of Saints have a priority over other celebrations. Sometimes there are options for the same day. The various celebrations are designated by the following titles, in order of importance: "Solemnity"; "Feast"; "Memorial"; "Optional Memorial." Sundays usually take precedence over other feast days, except for Solemnities and Feasts of the Lord.

Five "Proper Prayers" are included in every Mass: the Entrance Antiphon, the Opening Prayer (also called the Collect), the Prayer over the Offerings, the Communion Antiphon, and the Prayer after Communion. In addition, the First (and Second) Reading, the Responsorial Psalm, the Alleluia Verse, and the Gospel are "Proper Parts" of every Mass.

The "Ordinary Prayers" of the Mass are those prayers which are prayed throughout every celebration of the Mass and are almost always the same, except for certain omissions or adaptations for special occasions or for the various seasons or feast days during the Liturgical year, such as Christmas, Easter, Pentecost, etc. They are distinguished from the "Proper Prayers" of the Mass, which change from day to day.

[2] New American Catholic Edition The Holy Bible Confraternity Version, Benziger Brothers, Inc. New York, Boston, Cincinnati, Chicago, San Francisco, 1961; Copyrights by the Confraternity of Christian Doctrine and Benziger Brothers. (See also footnote 1, p. 35.)

[3] The following Psalms contain the word Alleluia:

104	112	117	147
105	113	118	148
106	114	136	149
111	116	146	150

4 In our western world the designations "B.C." and "A.D." are commonly used to indicate those periods of world history which took place either before the coming of Christ or beginning with the time of Christ and thereafter. These initials indicate the English phrase "before Christ (BC)" and the Latin phrase "anno domini(AD)," which is usually translated into English as "in the year of the Lord," but which also is sometimes simply referred to as "after Christ."

In the text related to this footnote, I have indicated that Jesus was conceived and then born in "approximately 4B.C." Obviously, this cannot mean that Jesus himself was born four years before his own birth. Then why do I speak of Jesus as being born in "approximately 4 B.C."? As a matter of fact, the exact date of Jesus' birth, even as to the year, is not known. Scholars have differing opinions based on the study of ancient calendars, various Scripture passages (Matthew 2,1-16; Luke 1,5-38; Luke 2,1-3;

Luke 3, 1 & 23; John 8,57), and other ancient writings. Considered dates for his birth range between 7BC and 2BC. In his book, *Jesus of Nazareth: the Infancy Narratives,* published in 2012, Pope Benedict XVI observed that the birth of Jesus was several years earlier than traditionally believed.

5 See <u>The Church Teaches</u>, Page 167, # 399. (See also the reference at the end of footnote 2 on page 19.)

6 The "Communion of Saints" is the only article of belief in the Apostles' Creed which is not expressed also in the Profession of Faith. It refers to the unity of all members of the Catholic Church on earth, in purgatory, and in heaven. This unity is such that there is among all members of the Church a power of intercession for one another through prayer, and a sharing by all in the holiness of the entire Church. Thus, Catholics on earth, by their prayers and good works can assist the souls in purgatory to gain more quickly full union with God

in heaven. And the souls in purgatory and the Saints in heaven, by their prayers and merits, can assist those members of the Church still living on earth towards greater holiness and in other ways.

[7] Below are English translations of the early Professions of Faith as they are found on pages 1,2,3, and 7 in The Church Teaches (See also the reference at end of footnote 2 on page 19).

Council of Nicaea: We believe in one God, the Father almighty, creator of all things both visible and invisible. And in one Lord Jesus Christ, the Son of God, the Only Begotten born of the Father, that is, of the substance of the Father; God from God, light from light, true God from true God; begotten, not created, consubstantial with the Father; through him all things were made, those in heaven and those on earth as well. For the sake of us men and for our salvation, he came down, was made flesh, and became man; he suffered and on the third day arose; he ascended into heaven and is going to come to judge the living and the dead. And we believe in the Holy Spirit.

As for those who say: "There was a time when he did not exist"; and, "Before he was begotten, he did not exist"; and, "He was made from nothing, or from another hypostasis or essence," alleging that the Son of God is mutable or subject to change —such persons the Catholic and apostolic Church condemns.

The Niceno-Constantinopolitan Creed: We believe in one God, the Father almighty, creator of heaven and earth, of all things both visible and invisible. And in one Lord Jesus Christ, the Only Begotten Son of God, born of the Father before all time; light from light, true God from true God; begotten, not created, consubstantial with the Father; through him all things were made. For the sake of us men and for our salvation, he came down from heaven, was made flesh by the Holy Spirit from the Virgin Mary, and became man; and he was crucified for our sake under Pontius Pilate, suffered, and was buried. And on the third day he arose according to the Scriptures; he ascended into heaven, sits at the right hand of the Father, and is going to come again in glory to judge the living and the dead. His reign will have no end. We believe in the Holy Spirit, the Lord, the giver of life; he proceeds from the Father, is adored and honored together with the Father and the Son; he spoke through the prophets. We believe in one, holy, Catholic, and apostolic Church. We profess one baptism for the forgiveness of sins. We expect the resurrection of the dead and the life of the world to come. Amen.

Council of Trent: I believe in one God, the Father almighty, maker of heaven and earth, and of all things visible and invisible; and in one Lord Jesus Christ, the Only Begotten Son of God, born of the Father before all ages; God from God, light from light, true God from true God; begotten not made, of one substance with the Father; through whom all things were made; who for us men and for our salvation came down from heaven, and was made incarnate by the Holy Spirit of the Virgin Mary, and was made man. He was crucified also for us under Pontius Pilate, died, and was buried; and he rose again the third day according to the Scriptures, and ascended into heaven; he sits at the right hand of the Father, and he shall come again in glory to judge the living and the dead, and of his kingdom there will be no end. And I believe in the Holy Spirit, the Lord, and giver of life, who proceeds from the Father and the Son; who equally with the Father and the Son is adored and glorified; who spoke through the prophets. And I believe that there is one, holy, Catholic, and apostolic Church. I confess one baptism for the remission of sins; and I hope for the resurrection of the dead, and the life of the world to come. Amen.

8 Here are some Scripture passages referring to Old Testament prophecies about the Resurrection of Jesus:

Luke 24, 25-27: Then he (Jesus) said to them, "What little sense you have! How slow you are to believe all that the prophets have announced! Did not the Messiah have to undergo all this so as to enter into his glory?" Beginning then with Moses and all the prophets, he interpreted for them every passage of Scripture which referred to him.

Acts 2, 29-32: Brothers, I (Peter) can speak confidently to you about our father David....He was a prophet and knew that God had sworn to him that one of his descendants would sit upon his throne.

He said that he was not abandoned to the nether world, nor did his body undergo corruption, thus proclaiming beforehand the resurrection of the Messiah. This is the Jesus God has raised up, and we are his witnesses.

Psalm 16, 8-10: I set the Lord ever before me; with him at my right hand I shall not be disturbed. Therefore my heart is glad and my soul rejoices, my body, too, abides in confidence; Because you will not abandon my soul to the nether world, nor will you suffer your faithful one to undergo corruption.

[9] **Matt. 28, 18-20:** Jesus came forward and addressed them in these words: "Full authority has been given to me both in heaven and on earth; go, therefore, and make disciples of all the nations. Baptize them in the name 'of the Father, and of the Son, and of the Holy Spirit.' Teach them to carry out everything I have commanded you. And know that I am with you always, until the end of the world!"

[10] For a deeper understanding of what it means to say that the Church is "one" and "catholic," consider the following passages from sections 13, 14, and 15 of the Dogmatic Constitution on the Church, Lumen Gentium, (issued by the Second Vatican Council in November, 1964; Flannery, Vol. 1, pgs.364 & 365; see footnote 1, pg. 35):

(Page 364) "13. All men are called to belong to the new People of God. This People therefore, whilst remaining one and only one, is to be spread throughout the whole world and to all ages in order that the design of God's will may be fulfilled: he made human nature one in the beginning and has decreed that all his children who were scattered should be finally gathered together as one (cf. John 11:52). It was for this purpose that God sent his Son, whom he appointed heir of all things (cf. Heb. 1:2), that he might be teacher, king and priest of all, the head of the new and universal People of God's sons. This, too, is why God sent the Spirit of his Son, the Lord and Giver of Life. The Spirit is, for the Church and for each and every believer, the principle of their union and unity in the teaching of the apostles and fellowship, in the breaking of bread and prayer (cf. Acts 2:42 Gk.).

"The one People of God is accordingly present in all the nations of the earth, since its citizens, who are taken from all nations, are of a kingdom whose nature is not earthly but heavenly."

(Page 365) "All men are called to this catholic unity which prefigures and promotes universal peace. And in different ways to it belong, or are related: the Catholic faithful, others who believe in Christ, and finally all mankind, called by God's grace to salvation."

(Page 366) "14. ...Fully incorporated into the Church are those who, possessing the Spirit of Christ, accept all the means of salvation given to the Church together with her entire organization, and who – by the bonds constituted by the profession of faith, the sacraments, ecclesiastical government, and communion –are joined in the visible structure of the Church of Christ, who rules her through the Supreme Pontiff and the bishops."...

"15. The Church knows that she is joined in many ways to the baptized who are honored by the name of Christian, but who do not however profess the Catholic faith in its entirety or have not preserved unity or communion under the successor of Peter."

CHAPTER SIX

THINK ABOUT IT

Various Reflections Related to
the Real Presence of Jesus in the Eucharist

In this final chapter of the book, I would like to share several insights and reflections which have come to me over the years. In one way or another, these reflections have something to do with the Real Presence of Jesus in the Eucharist.

Jesus remains on earth in the Eucharist

The one and only Jesus Christ was (is) on earth in two ways: 1. in his natural existence on earth with his disciples and others of his time (approximately 4B.C.- 33A.D.) 2. with the rest of us human beings—including those of us in this 21st century A.D.— in the Eucharist.

Consider the following passage from St. John's Gospel: *Jesus said to them: I solemnly assure you, it was not Moses who gave you bread from the heavens; it is my Father who gives you the real heavenly bread. God's bread comes down from heaven and gives life to the world."* **(John 6, 32-33)**

The manna "fell from heaven" and fed the people. All over the world, Jesus literally gives life to people as they eat the bread of the Eucharist. Just as people eat food every day, all over the world, to sustain their bodily lives, so Jesus, all over the world every day sustains the spiritual lives of those who eat of him in the Eucharistic bread—not in the future, but here and now throughout their lives on earth.

God sent Jesus into the world as the Bread of Life –to nourish the world with Divine Life –not just during the 3 years of his public life or even the 33 years of his entire natural life on this earth; but for all people of all times since Jesus lived his natural life on earth. As far as we know, (The New Testament certainly makes no mention of it) during his natural existence on earth, Jesus never travelled, as an adult, beyond the general area of the Holy Land; and so he was limited in his presence on earth, and particularly during his public life, to an area approximately 90 miles long and 30 miles wide, more or less in the same geographical area as the modern-day country of Israel. So, in a way, it seems true to say that Jesus accomplishes the mission given Him by the Father more widely and extensively and over a longer period of time in and through and by means of His Eucharistic Presence on earth, than he did by his natural way of living on earth, from his conception until his death, centuries ago.

But don't forget—it was precisely his life on earth and his death, accepted in total love and obedience, by which Jesus actually redeemed us, that is, saved us from eternal death and gave us eternal life. Jesus seems to "apply" this salvation to human beings through the Eucharist: "He who eats my flesh and drinks my blood has eternal life, and I will raise him up on the last day."**(John 6, 54)** And He instituted the Eucharist on the night before his death and in explicit relationship to that death.

I am with you always

At the Last supper, as we read in St. John's Gospel, Jesus says, *"I will not leave you orphaned; I will come back to you."*(**John 14, 18**) And just before his ascension into heaven, as we read in St. Matthew's Gospel, Jesus said to his apostles, *"Know that I am with you always until the end of the world!"*(**Matt. 28, 20**)

In both instances these words of Jesus were directed to his Apostles; but they would live on earth only another several decades. And so, the words of Jesus in St. Matthew's Gospel seem to be directed even more to us who live on earth twenty centuries later. Was he not, in effect, saying to all those who would follow him on earth, including us, "Don't think of me as 'being in the past.' Yes, I lived a natural existence on earth early in the first century; but I, the same Jesus, am with you now as much as I was with my Apostles—in a different way, but truly and really. Just as I sat at the Last Supper with the Apostles and others, so—in the celebration of the Eucharist and in tabernacles all over the world—I, the same Jesus, am just as really with you and sit with you, down through the centuries. And I am with you for the same reasons: to console you, to strengthen you, and especially to reveal to you our Father's love. For He is your Father, too, just as truly,—not by nature, but by creation and adoption—as He is mine."

The identity of Jesus with the Father in relation to the Eucharist

When I compare the discourse given by Jesus in chapter six of St. John's Gospel with the discourse of Jesus at the Last Supper in chapter fourteen; and then consider that these latter words of Jesus were spoken on the same occasion on which He instituted the Eucharist, I can't help wondering whether Jesus' words on both occasions were intended to give us a deeper and fuller understanding of why He instituted the Eucharist. In both discourses, Jesus seems to relate his giving us the Eucharist to his own relationship with the Father. Consider the following passages from the two discourses:

JOHN 6 (Discourse at Capernaum)

6, 32: "...It is My Father who gives you the real heavenly bread."

6, 33: "God's bread comes down from heaven and gives life to the world."

6, 35: "...I myself am the bread of life."

6, 44: "No one can come to me unless the Father who sent me draws him;"...

6, 45: "Everyone who has heard the Father and learned from him comes to me."

6, 46: "Not that anyone has seen the Father –only the one who is from God has seen the Father."

6, 57: "Just as the Father who has life sent me and I have life because of the Father, so the man who feeds on me will have life because of me."

JOHN 14 (Discourse at Last Supper/Eucharist)

14, 6: "I am the way the truth, and the life, no one comes to the Father but through me."

14, 7: "If you really knew me you would know my Father also. From this point on you know him; you have seen him."

14, 9: "Whoever has seen me has seen the Father."

14, 10: "Do you not believe that I am in the Father and the Father is in me?"

14, 11: "Believe me that I am in the Father and the Father is in me,..."

14, 20: "On that day you will know that I am in my Father and you in me, and I in you."

14, 23: "Anyone who loves me will be true to my word, and my Father will love him; we will come to him and make our dwelling place with him."

In these passages, Jesus seems to link his identity with the Father with his presence in the Eucharist. Especially when we consider **John 6, 57**—*"Just as the Father who has life sent me and I have life because of the Father, so the man who feeds on me will have life because of me"; and* **John 14, 20,** *"On that day you will know that I am in my Father and you in me, and I in you."*—we are led to the conclusion (or at least to ask the question), "Did Jesus institute the Eucharist, not simply as a means of joining us to himself in a special union, but even more so in order to draw us into his own Trinitarian Unity with the Father and the Holy Spirit?" In other words, when we receive Holy Communion, it is a relationship not just between "Jesus and me," but between the "Father, Son Incarnate, with the Holy Spirit, and me."

The Presence of Jesus in the tabernacle

With full belief and granted the real presence of Jesus in the tabernacle, there is no visible indication of His presence (other than a sanctuary light) nor of his action in our lives due to this special presence. He seems to "just be there." And yet, there is, in fact, a hidden but real action of Jesus in our spiritual lives through his reserved Eucharistic presence in the tabernacle. He is there for the same reason He appeared to the apostles in the upper room after his resurrection, namely to console and strengthen us and give us a vibrant hope of our own eternal life someday with Him in Heaven; and to give us His grace and to assure us, in the meantime, of His efficacious presence in our lives on earth.

But since Jesus does all this for us in such a silent, hidden manner, by "just being there," is it not an acceptable and praiseworthy form of prayer in our visits before the Blessed Sacrament to "just be there" with Him, even if we do not pray specific prayers (which, of course, are also totally acceptable during such visits)? We may sit silently, quietly warding off distracting thoughts by simply gazing at the tabernacle and momentarily recalling His presence within.

Some thoughts concerning the death of Jesus

In St. John's Gospel, in a conversation between Jesus and the Pharisees, Jesus, among other things, said to them,

"I am the good shepherd. I know my sheep...for these sheep I will give my life. ...The Father loves me for this: that I lay down my life to take it up again. No one takes it from me; I lay it down freely. I have power to lay it down, and I have power to take it up again. This command I received from my Father." **(John 10: 11, 14, 15, 17, 18)**

From these words of Jesus one might infer that Jesus did not have to die. And it would seem that by reason of his Hypostatic Union with God the Son, at the very least, Jesus surely could have avoided passing through human death.

On the other hand, when we consider that death is a necessary part of being human in a fallen world, and since Jesus was like us in all things except sin, it seems that Jesus had to die in one way or another. However, the manner and time of his death could have been different from what they were, without changing the fact of his death as someone fully human in a fallen world.

Therefore, the above words of Jesus in St. John's Gospel might be taken both to refer to the fact that Jesus freely chose not to miraculously avoid human death; and also, even more importantly, to the freedom, love, and obedience to his Father with which he fully embraced death at the time and manner in which it happened to him.

St. Paul's words in his Letter to the Philippians seem to confirm this:

> *"Though he was in the form of God, he did not deem equality with God something to be grasped at. Rather, he emptied himself and took the form of a slave, being born in the likeness of men. He was known to be of human estate, and it was thus that he humbled himself, obediently accepting even death, death on a cross!"* **(Phil. 2, 6-8)**

Again, in his Letter to the Romans, Paul speaks of the relationship between sin, death, and the redeeming death of Jesus:

> *"Therefore, just as through one man sin entered the world and with sin death, death thus coming to all men inasmuch as all sinned. ..."* **(Rm. 5, 12)** and, *"Just as through one man's disobedience all became sinners, so through one man's obedience all shall become just."* **(Rm. 5, 19)**

We find a similar thought expressed in **1 Peter 2, 24**: *In his* *own body he brought your sins to the cross. . ."*

And so, Jesus not only accepts his death as a full member of the fallen human race, but, in total love and obedience to His Father, he embraces it fully with all its ignominy, pain, and suffering; and so, because of his free and obedient acceptance, the death of Jesus becomes the sole human act in all of human history which redeems the whole human race from the effects of sin and death.

Consider for a moment what the ordinary experience of death is for every human being. In itself, death is the human person's nemesis, his greatest obstacle, his <u>end</u>. Death is experienced as the extermination of one's life, the dissolution of one's being. But Jesus, by accepting death in total love and obedience to the Father and then rising from death, gives all human beings an example of overcoming death. He proves that man can and does live on after actual death. The resurrection of Jesus from death, in fact, is the primary basis human beings have on which to base their hope of the resurrection of their own bodies after death. When in turn we accept faith in the future resurrection of our own bodies, death becomes for us the ultimate and supreme opportunity for us to express our total belief and trust in God, and our total obedience to Him, in imitation of Jesus.

Since in every Mass we join Jesus in the eternal moment of his total, obedient surrender in death to God, our participation in each Mass with our effort to surrender ourselves totally to God along with Jesus, becomes for us, as it were, a "dress rehearsal" for the moment of our own death, whenever it may come to us.

Here is another thought about the death of Jesus: Jesus not only died—as he chose to do, being fully human in a fallen world—but he died a very drawn-out, painful, ignominious death as a publicly-condemned criminal, including the scourging at the pillar, the crowning with thorns, and the carrying of his own cross. For our sake he wholeheartedly embraced one of the worst possible ways for a human being to experience death, in such a prolonged and excruciating manner.

To use the words once spoken to me by a retreat director (Fr. Edward O'Brien, S.J.), "The God who exists in a way beyond the way everything I know and experience exists, has become fully human and died this way as a response to sin (original, mine, everyone's) to save us from that sin and its eternal effects. I— we—other human beings are incapable of saving ourselves."

Through baptism into the death of Christ, however, we gain this salvation:

"Are you not aware that we who were baptized into Christ Jesus were baptized into his death? Through baptism into his death we were buried with him, so that, just as Christ was raised from the dead by the glory of the Father, we too might live a new life." **(Rm. 6, 3-4)**.

St. Thomas Aquinas also expresses this beautifully: "For since He is our head, then, by the Passion which He endured from love and obedience, He delivered us as His members from our sins, as by the price of His Passion: in the same way as if a man by the good industry of his hands were to redeem himself from a sin committed with his feet. For, just as the natural body is one, though made up of diverse members, so the whole Church, Christ's mystic body, is reckoned as one person with its head, which is Christ." (Summa Theologica, part III, q.49, a.1). (Benziger Brothers edition, volume two, pg. 2288; see footnote #3, p.36.)

In addition to the above reasons that help us understand why Jesus had to die—which are based simply on the facts of our fallen human existence—there is also another very important "liturgical" reason for his death. Remember that all through the history of God's People during the Old Testament, their relationship with God was repeatedly ratified and confirmed through covenants which involved shedding the blood of animals sacrificed to God. Remember, too, that in instituting the Eucharist Jesus said that he was giving the apostles his body which would be "given up" and his blood of the new and eternal covenant which would be "poured out" for the forgiveness of sin. Jesus Himself, then, spoke of his death on Calvary as a sacrifice in which his blood would be shed.

St. Paul, the other Apostles, and the first Christians understood Jesus' death on the cross to be the shedding of blood and the sacrificial death—not of an animal, but of Jesus Himself – which established the final covenant with God, in which all men were freed from sin and death and given the promise of eternal life. Besides the passage quoted above (p. 127) from St. Paul's Letter to the Romans, we find this idea expressed repeatedly in the following Scripture passages:

Colossians 1, 19-20 and 22: *It pleased God to make absolute fullness reside in him and, by means of him, to reconcile everything in his person, both on earth and in the heavens, making peace through the blood of his cross. ...But now Christ has achieved reconciliation for you in his mortal body by dying, so as to present you to God holy, free of reproach and blame."*

Ephesians 2, 16: *reconciling both of us to God in one body through his cross. ...*

Hebrews 2, 9: *but we do see Jesus crowned with glory and honor because he suffered death: Jesus, who was made for a little while lower than the angels, that through God's gracious will he might taste death for the sake of all men.*

Again, too, John the Baptist called Jesus *the Lamb of God* **(John 1, 36)**, and the Book of Revelation speaks of him as the Lamb of sacrifice:

> *Then, between the throne with the four living creatures and the elders, I saw a Lamb standing, a Lamb that had been <u>slain</u>. ...The Lamb came and received the scroll from the right hand of the One who sat on the throne. ... "Worthy are you to receive the scroll and break open its seals, for you were <u>slain</u>. With your blood you purchased for God men of every race and tongue, of every people and nation. You made of them a kingdom, and priests to serve our God, and they shall reign on the earth."* **(Rev. 5: 6,7, 9,10)**

And so, as the culmination of God's plan of revelation in bringing about the salvation of all human beings through a history of covenants and sacrifice, Jesus, the Messiah, must die as the Lamb of Sacrifice, hung upon the cross, thus establishing the new and eternal covenant of the human race with God. How appropriate that in our own liturgical celebration of the Mass, as soon as Jesus becomes present on the altar in the eternal moment of his redeeming death, we respond with the words, "We proclaim your Death, O Lord, and profess your Resurrection until you come again."

I conclude the reflections of this final chapter by repeating one more time the comment which I have made several times earlier in these pages: "What a magnificent and most marvelous gift our God has given us Catholics in the Real Presence of Jesus in the Eucharist!"

Ascension, Francisco Camilo, 1651, courtesy of Wikimedia,
https://commons.wikimedia.org/wiki/File:Francisco_Camilo_-
Ascension-_Google_Art_Project.jpg

APPENDIX I

WHAT'S THAT WORD?

An Explanation of Some Words That Are Found in Prayers of the Mass or in Church Documents

Note: the explanations of the words which are given below are not strictly definitions of the words as such—although an explicit definition may at times be included; rather, these are explanations of the meanings of the words as they are used in various places in this book. The number (or numbers), which are in parentheses beside each word, indicate the more important page or pages where the word is used in the book. In the text itself a word which is explained in this Appendix is marked with an asterisk. However, when the same word appears repeatedly, it is not marked with the asterisk every time.

accident (12, 20, 21)

The meaning of this word has nothing to do with the expression "It was an accident." Rather, it is a technical word used in the study of the Philosophy of Being, which refers to that component of any existing thing by reason of which that thing is able to change in various ways while still remaining essentially the same thing. A fuller explanation of this word is given in the text and in footnote 3 for chapter one of this book.

(See also the explanation of <u>substance</u> at the end of this list of words.)

<u>anathema</u> (8, 19)

This word originally comes from a Greek word meaning "dedicated." It is used in Scripture to mean something "dedicated to evil and therefore accursed." In Church documents, it is used in a technical sense as part of the official formula which declares that someone is excommunicated from the Catholic Church for refusing to believe a doctrine which is essential to the Catholic Faith.

<u>begotten</u> (79, 90, 96-100, 115, 116)

To be "begotten" means to come from something else. This word is usually used to indicate that a baby gets its existence from its father and mother: Parents "beget" a child, or their child is "begotten" by them. The phrase, "the Only Begotten Son of God," refers to the fact that, in the mystery of the Blessed Trinity, God the Son comes from God the Father. The Father generates the Son. However, the Father has no kind of union with another person in order to generate the Son (as in human generation, which is also called "conception"). Furthermore, in God there is no time sequence of any kind, but, from all eternity the uncreated God exists simultaneously as Father begetting the Son and the Holy Spirit proceeding from the Father and the Son.

<u>catholic</u> (19, 35, 64, 97, 104, 117, 118)

When the word "Catholic," with a capital "C" is used today, most people correctly understand it as a reference which distinguishes Catholics, as members of the Catholic Church, from members of other Christian (and even non-Christian) Churches or religions. However, the original meaning of the word <u>catholic</u> is simply "universal," that is, something which is found everywhere. In Matthew's Gospel Jesus told his Apostles, "Full authority has been given to me both in heaven and on earth; go, therefore, and make disciples of all the nations" (Mt. 28:18-19).

And so the Church founded by the Apostles of Jesus is said to be "catholic." We read in the Acts of the Apostles that those who accepted and began to follow the teaching of the Apostles about Jesus were first called "Christians" in the city of Antioch, in Syria. (Acts, 12:26). St. Ignatius of Antioch used the expression "catholic church" in his letter to the Smyrnaeans early in the second century A.D, and St. Cyril of Jerusalem also spoke of the "catholic church" during the 4th century A.D.

Although it is very widely used today, the phrase "Catholic Church" (spelled with its capital "C") first became more significant in light of the separation between Catholic Christians and Orthodox Christians in 1054A.D (even though the official title of the Orthodox Church is the "Orthodox Catholic Church"). The use of the word "Catholic" became still more significant in distinguishing the Catholic Church from other Christian Churches after the various Protestant Churches separated from Catholic Christianity in 1517AD. In 1908, to distinguish the Catholic Church even more clearly from other Christian Churches which are not in full communion with the Catholic Church, Pope St. Pius X referred to the latter as the "Roman Catholic Church."

In the Profession of Faith proclaimed by Catholics during the celebration of Sunday Mass ("I believe in one, holy, catholic and apostolic Church") the word catholic is not capitalized and is used in its original sense of "universal."

confess (105, 116)

This word is used in two different ways in the Catholic Church. It usually refers to the Sacrament of Penance, or Reconciliation, in which a person confesses his or her sins to a priest in order to receive God's forgiveness. This action is also known as "Going to Confession." This use of the word usually implies the idea of revealing something that has been hidden or secret and for which a person feels a sense of guilt. However, in a totally different usage, the word <u>confess</u> can also mean the same thing as the word <u>profess</u>, that is, to "declare or to proclaim one's belief" in some truth. This latter use of the word, of course, has nothing to do with "going to Confession," "having sorrow for sin," "secrecy, "or "guilt." Quite the contrary, to "confess" one's belief is to proclaim it openly for others to hear. It is in this sense that the word <u>confess</u> is used in the Profession of Faith ("I confess one Baptism for the forgiveness of sins.")

<u>coheirs</u> (63)

An "heir" is someone who inherits something. A "coheir" is someone who inherits something along with someone else; they share an inheritance. "Coheirs" is the plural form of "coheir." In Eucharistic Prayer II, we are asking God to let us share the inheritance of Heaven along with all the other persons who have gone to Heaven.

<u>minister</u> (43, 44, 59, 61)

As a noun, "minister" refers to someone who in some way serves or helps another person. It is often used in reference to a person who is the pastor of a church or who is engaged in religious ceremonies. As a verb, "minister" refers to the actual act of serving someone. One person "ministers" to another in some way, by providing some kind of service to them. The use of this word in Eucharistic Prayer II is further discussed on page 56 in the text of this book.

<u>perceptible</u> (8, 14, 22)

This word means that something is visible; it is not hidden, but rather it can be seen or heard or felt or smelled or tasted or known intellectually; it is noticeable.

prescriptions (31)

This word can have different meanings. We often use it with reference to a medicine which a doctor has prescribed for our use. Another meaning however is "rules" or "regulations" or "laws," that is, something which is "prescribed for us to do or to obey. That is the meaning of "prescriptions" in this passage from the Letter to the Hebrews.

paten (58)

The "paten" is the small plate on which the large host is placed (sometimes along with small hosts) for consecration during the Mass. During the Preparation of Gifts, the priest holds up the paten in offering the bread to God; afterwards he places it on the altar next to the chalice which contains the wine to be consecrated.

species (8, 14, 16, 22, 59)

This word, often used in relation to the word genus, ordinarily means "kinds" of things, as in the expression, "There are many species of animals." In this document of the Council of Trent, however, and on the following pages which discuss Trent's teaching, "species" has a very special and particular (even technical) meaning. It is an alternative word used for the word "accidents" (explained above) and refers specifically to the accidents of bread and wine which remain after the substances (explained below) of the same bread and wine have been changed into the substances of the body and blood of Jesus by the celebrant's words of Consecration. After the Consecration of the Mass, when we look at the "consecrated hosts" on the paten (or in a ciborium) and the "consecrated wine" in the chalice, we refer to them as the "sacred species." What our eyes see are only the "accidents" or "species" of bread and wine, without their former substances, which have now become "the whole Christ, body and blood, soul and divinity." Another word which could be used to describe what we see, is "appearances" of bread and wine. *Webster's Seventh New Collegiate Dictionary* gives as definition 2 of the word <u>species</u>, "the consecrated Eucharistic elements; specif: the accidents of the Eucharistic bread and wine as distinguished in Roman Catholicism from their substance."

<u>substance</u> (8, 11, 20, 21)

Like the word <u>accident,</u> at the beginning of this list, "substance" is a technical word used in the study of the Philosophy of Being. Again, its meaning is much more limited than the ordinary meaning of the word "substance" as "a thing of some kind," like a "thick substance," or the expression, "There is no substance to what he says," etc. "Substance" is used in connection with the philosophical term "accident" and indicates that component in the make-up of any existing thing by reason of which that thing always remains essentially the same thing, even though it undergoes many "accidental" changes. This word is discussed at length both in the text and in footnote 3 for chapter one of this book.

APPENDIX II

FIRST HOLY COMMUNION

Some Reflections on Preparing Children for their First Holy Communion

In no least way do I claim to be a specialist on the subject of preparing children for their First Holy Communion, and I am sure that there are many people who are much more qualified than I am to undertake this task. Although I hesitate to write on the subject, I thought that perhaps the following reflections might be of some help to those teachers who do have this responsibility.

When I was pastor (1987-1990) at Mount Carmel Church in Pueblo, CO, the nephew of one of my parishioners was being prepared for his First Holy Communion in another parish. When the teacher told the children that they would eat the Body of Christ and drink his Blood, the boy replied, "Yuk! I don't want to make my First Communion."

Many years earlier (shortly after Vatican II), while I was teaching religion at Rockhurst High School in Kansas City, Missouri, I was one of several priests who used to celebrate special parish Masses that were prepared by a group of lay men and women known as "The Contemporary Mass Group." Their efforts were aimed at facilitating the implementation of those changes in the liturgy of the Mass which had been legislated by the Second Vatican Council.

On one of these occasions, after the celebration of Mass had taken place, I was standing in the sanctuary along with a few other persons. One of them was the daughter, about 5 years old, of one of the members of the Mass Group. She pointed to the tabernacle and asked me, "What is in there?" It so happened that I still had the tabernacle key in my pocket. So, without saying a word in answer to her question, I picked her up, opened the tabernacle, and let her look in. Then I closed the tabernacle and put her down. And that was the end of it. She did not ask any further questions.

I have often reflected that had I answered her question by saying, "Jesus is in there," or "That's where Jesus lives," not only would I not have satisfied her curiosity, but I would have created unnecessary problems in her young imagination and mind. Remember, again, my student's problem about squeezing a man into a Host.

It is good to know that the Church's Code of Canon Law, in speaking of "Participation in the Blessed Eucharist," reads as follows in Canon no. 913:

"# 1. For holy communion to be administered to children, it is required that they have <u>sufficient knowledge</u> and be accurately prepared, so that <u>according to their capacity</u> they understand what the mystery of Christ means, and are able to receive the Body of the Lord with faith and devotion."

"#2. The Blessed Eucharist may, however, be administered to children in danger of death <u>if they can distinguish the Body of Christ from ordinary food</u> and receive communion with reverence."

I have underlined certain words in the above passage quoted from Canon Law, because I think they are of great importance.

In order that they might become able to receive Communion with faith and reverent devotion, children being prepared for First Holy Communion need to be given sufficient knowledge according to their capacity. They need not—indeed, they cannot—be taught the more complete comprehension of the Eucharist which they will be able to understand once they have grown to adulthood. Such fuller understanding requires the ability to engage in abstract reasoning, an ability which children of the usual First Communion age do not yet have. So, for example, a teacher should not try to present to children the concept of "substance" which the *Decree on the Most Holy Eucharist* uses in its teaching about the Eucharist.

On the other hand, it is good to remember that in declaring the truth of the doctrine of the Real presence of Jesus in the Eucharist, the words used by the *Decree on the Most Holy Eucharist* are that Jesus "is <u>contained</u> under the perceptible species of bread and wine." These words used by the *Decree* suggest that Jesus is somehow "within," or "inside of" what continues to look and taste and feel like bread and wine. But it is completely different from ordinary bread and wine, because Jesus is "substantially" present within it. Moreover, since the presence of Jesus in the Eucharist is real but is not the natural way he exists in Heaven, children should be cautioned not to try to understand or imagine how Jesus is present in the consecrated host or wine, but simply to believe that Jesus himself, through God's miraculous power, really comes to them when they receive the Host in Holy Communion. There is no way they can truly picture in their minds the manner of His presence.

The teacher might consider using words similar to the following:

"When the priest prays the words of Consecration over the bread and wine, they change from being ordinary bread and

139

wine—even though they still look like it—into a very different and special kind of bread-like food and drink which actually contain Jesus himself, with his whole being: body and blood, soul, and divinity. But he is present there in a very special, miraculous, different, and hidden way of existing, not like the way he naturally existed when he was on earth or the way he naturally exists now in heaven. And so there is no way for us to imagine how he is there. But, when we receive Holy Communion, Jesus truly and really does come within us in this special way, even though we can't see Him and we don't feel anything different in ourselves except the natural taste of bread and wine."

Needless to say, it is easier to talk about "what not to say" than about "what should be said."

Another reflection which may be of some help to those who prepare children for their First Holy Communion concerns the use of the word <u>bread</u> to refer to the Body of Christ after the change which is brought about by the Words of Consecration. Some persons seem uncomfortable in referring to the consecrated Host as "Bread." They seem to feel obliged always to use the words "the Body of Christ," (and "the Blood of Christ") in referring to the Eucharist, even when the context in which they are speaking causes a certain awkwardness in the use of these words.

Perhaps such persons would feel more at ease, were they to consider the fact that, even after the Words of Consecration, the Eucharistic Prayers of the Mass themselves refer to Christ in his real, true, and total presence in the Eucharist as "Bread." For example, Eucharistic Prayer I speaks of, "the holy *Bread* of eternal life and the *Chalice* of everlasting salvation." Likewise, in the prayer following the Consecration, Eucharistic Prayer II refers to "the *Bread* of life and the *Chalice* of salvation." And Eucharistic Prayer IV uses the words "to all who partake of this one *Bread* and one *Chalice*." Of course, after the Words of Consecration these same prayers also make reference to the *Body and Blood* of Jesus; and the truth of this reality is unhesitatingly presumed in all of the other expressions listed above.

In addition, in one of the options given for the acclamation of the congregation after Jesus becomes present in the Eucharist through the Words of Consecration, the people pray, "When we eat this *Bread* and drink this *Cup*, we proclaim your death, O Lord, until you come again."

The Church, always presuming the truth of the real presence of Jesus in the Eucharist, nonetheless, in its many documents and hymns, in addition to the words "the Body and Blood of Christ," uses a variety of other titles in referring to this miraculous reality. Here are some of them:

The Blessed Sacrament
The Real Presence
Holy Communion
Sacred Host
Consecrated Host
Consecrated Wine
The Consecrated Bread and Wine
The Sacred Species
The Holy Sacrament of the Altar
Saving Victim
Living Bread
Life-Giving Bread
Bread of Life
Bread from Heaven
Bread Eternal
The Eucharist
Bread Blessed and Broken (hymn)
Gift of Finest Wheat (hymn)

Let us conclude by recalling once more the words of the *Decree on the Most Holy Eucharist:* "...*in the blessed sacrament of the Holy Eucharist, after the consecration of the bread and wine, Our Lord Jesus Christ, true God and man, is truly, really, and substantially contained under the perceptible species of bread and wine...We can hardly find words to express this way of existing; but our reason, guided by faith, can know that it is possible for God, and this we should always believe unhesitatingly.*"

APPENDIX III

EUCHARISTIC PRAYERS

The Four Ordinary Eucharist Prayers

[Note: These full texts of the Eucharistic Prayers (except for the prayers of acclamation after the Consecration and the special prayers in Masses for the dead) are provided for ready reference in reading chapters 3 & 4 of this book. The words in bold print are discussed in chapter 4.]

Eucharistic Prayer I

To you, therefore, most merciful Father, we make humble prayer and petition through Jesus Christ, your Son, our Lord: that you accept and bless these **gifts**, these **offerings**, these holy and unblemished **sacrifices**, which we offer you firstly for your holy catholic Church. Be pleased to grant her peace, to guard, unite and govern her throughout the whole world, together with your servant N. our Pope and N. our Bishop, and all those who, holding to the truth, hand on the catholic and apostolic faith.

Remember, Lord, your servants N. and N. and all gathered here, whose faith and devotion are known to you. For them, we offer you this **sacrifice** of praise or they offer it for themselves and all who are dear to them: for the redemption of their souls, in hope of health and well-being, and paying their homage to you, the eternal God, living and true.

In communion with those whose memory we venerate, especially the glorious ever-Virgin Mary, Mother of our God and Lord, Jesus Christ, and blessed Joseph, her Spouse, your blessed Apostles and Martyrs, Peter and Paul, Andrew, (James, John, Thomas, James, Philip, Bartholomew, Matthew, Simon and Jude; Linus, Cletus, Clement, Sixtus, Cornelius, Cyprian, Lawrence, Chrysogonus, John and Paul, Cosmas and Damian) and all your Saints; we ask that through their merits and prayers, in all things we may be defended by your protecting help. (Through Christ our Lord. Amen.)

Therefore, Lord, we pray: graciously accept this **oblation** of our service, that of your whole family; order our days in your peace, and command that we be delivered from eternal damnation and counted among the flock of those you have chosen. (Through Christ our Lord. Amen.)

Be pleased, O God, we pray, to bless, acknowledge, and approve this **offering** in every respect; make it spiritual and acceptable, so that it may become for us the Body and Blood of your most beloved Son, our Lord Jesus Christ.

On the day before he was to suffer, he took bread in his holy and venerable hands, and with eyes raised to heaven to you, O God, his almighty Father, giving you thanks, he said the blessing, broke the bread and gave it to his disciples, saying: TAKE THIS, ALL OF YOU, AND EAT OF IT, FOR THIS IS MY BODY, WHICH WILL BE GIVEN UP FOR YOU.

In a similar way, when supper was ended, he took this precious chalice in his holy and venerable hands, and once more giving you thanks, he said the blessing and gave the chalice to his disciples, saying: TAKE THIS, ALL OF YOU, AND DRINK FROM IT, FOR THIS IS THE CHALICE OF MY BLOOD, THE BLOOD OF THE NEW AND ETERNAL COVENANT, WHICH WILL BE POURED OUT FOR YOU AND FOR MANY FOR THE FORGIVENESS OF SINS. DO THIS IN MEMORY OF ME.

Therefore, O Lord, as we celebrate the memorial of the blessed Passion, the Resurrection from the dead, and the glorious Ascension into heaven of Christ, your Son, our Lord, we, your servants and your holy people, offer to your glorious majesty from the **gifts** that you have given us, this pure victim, this holy victim, this spotless victim, the holy Bread of eternal life and the Chalice of everlasting salvation.

Be pleased to look upon these **offerings** with a serene and kindly countenance, and to accept them, as once you were pleased to accept the gifts of your servant Abel the just, the sacrifice of Abraham, our father in faith, and the offering of your high priest Melchizedek, a holy **sacrifice,** a spotless **victim.**

In humble prayer we ask you, almighty God: command that these **gifts** be borne by the hands of your holy Angel to your altar on high in the sight of your divine majesty, so that all of us, who through this participation at the altar receive the most holy Body and Blood of your Son, may be filled with every grace and heavenly blessing. (Through Christ our Lord. Amen.)

Remember also, Lord, your servants N. and N., who have gone before us with the sign of faith and rest in the sleep of peace. Grant them, O Lord, we pray, and all who sleep in Christ, a place of refreshment, light and peace. (Through Christ our Lord. Amen.)

To us, also, your servants, who, though sinners, hope in your abundant mercies, graciously grant some share and fellowship with your holy Apostles and Martyrs: with John the Baptist, Stephen, Matthias, Barnabas, (Ignatius, Alexander, Marcellinus, Peter, Felicity, Perpetua, Agatha, Lucy, Agnes, Cecilia, Anastasia) and all your Saints; admit us, we beseech you, into their company, not weighing our merits, but granting us your pardon, through Christ our Lord.

Through whom you continue to make all these good things, O Lord; you sanctify them, fill them with life, bless them, and bestow them upon us.

Through him, and with him, and in him, O God, almighty Father, in the unity of the Holy Spirit, all glory and honor is yours, for ever and ever. (The people acclaim: Amen.)

Eucharistic Prayer II

You are indeed Holy, O Lord, the fount of all holiness. Make holy, therefore, these **gifts**, we pray, by sending down your Spirit upon them like the dewfall, so that they may become for us the Body and Blood of our Lord Jesus Christ. At the time he was betrayed and entered willingly into his Passion, he took bread and, giving thanks, broke it, and gave it to his disciples, saying: TAKE THIS, ALL OF YOU, AND EAT OF IT, FOR THIS IS MY BODY, WHICH WILL BE GIVEN UP FOR YOU.

In a similar way, when supper was ended, he took the chalice and, once more giving thanks, he gave it to his disciples, saying: TAKE THIS, ALL OF YOU, AND DRINK FROM IT, FOR THIS IS THE CHALICE OF MY BLOOD, THE BLOOD OF THE NEW AND ETERNAL COVENANT, WHICH WILL BE POURED OUT FOR YOU AND FOR MANY FOR THE FORGIVENESS OF

SINS. DO THIS IN MEMORY OF ME.

Therefore, as we celebrate the memorial of his Death and Resurrection, we offer you, Lord, the Bread of life and the Chalice of salvation, giving thanks that you have held us worthy to be in your presence and minister to you.

Humbly we pray that, partaking of the Body and Blood of Christ, we may be gathered into one by the Holy Spirit.

Remember, Lord, your Church, spread throughout the world, and bring her to the fullness of charity, together with N. our Pope and N. our Bishop and all the clergy.

Remember also our brothers and sisters who have fallen asleep in the hope of the resurrection, and all who have died in your mercy: welcome them into the light of your face. Have mercy on us all, we pray, that with the Blessed Virgin Mary, Mother of God, with blessed Joseph, her Spouse, with the blessed Apostles, and all the Saints who have pleased you throughout the ages, we may merit to be coheirs to eternal life, and may praise and glorify you through your Son, Jesus Christ.

Through him, and with him, and in him, O God, almighty Father, in the unity of the Holy Spirit, all glory and honor is yours, for ever and ever. (The people acclaim: Amen.)

Eucharistic Prayer III

You are indeed Holy, O Lord, and all you have created rightly gives you praise, for through your Son our Lord Jesus Christ, by the power and working of the Holy Spirit, you give life to all things and make them holy, and you never cease to gather a people to yourself, so that from the rising of the sun to its setting a pure **sacrifice** may be offered to your name.

Therefore, O Lord, we humbly implore you: by the same Spirit graciously make holy these **gifts** we have brought to you for consecration: that they may become the Body and Blood of your Son our Lord Jesus Christ, at whose command we celebrate these mysteries.

For on the night he was betrayed he himself took bread, and, giving you thanks, he said the blessing, broke the bread and gave it to his disciples, saying: TAKE THIS, ALL OF YOU, AND EAT OF IT, FOR THIS IS MY BODY, WHICH WILL BE GIVEN UP FOR YOU.

In a similar way, when supper was ended, he took the chalice, and, giving you thanks, he said the blessing, and gave the chalice to his disciples, saying: TAKE THIS, ALL OF YOU, AND DRINK FROM IT, FOR THIS IS THE CHALICE OF MY BLOOD, THE BLOOD OF THE NEW AND ETERNAL COVENANT, WHICH WILL BE POURED OUT FOR YOU AND FOR MANY FOR THE FORGIVENESS OF SINS. DO THIS IN MEMORY OF ME.

Therefore, O Lord, as we celebrate the memorial of the saving Passion of your Son, his wondrous Resurrection and Ascension into heaven, and as we look forward to his second coming, we offer you in thanksgiving this holy and living

sacrifice.

Look, we pray, upon the **oblation** of your Church and, recognizing the sacrificial Victim by whose death you willed to reconcile us to yourself, grant that we, who are nourished by the Body and Blood of your Son and filled with his Holy Spirit, may become one body, one spirit in Christ.

May he make of us an eternal **offering** to you, so that we may obtain an inheritance with your elect, especially with the most Blessed Virgin Mary, Mother of God, with blessed Joseph, her Spouse, with your blessed Apostles and glorious Martyrs (with Saint N.) and with all the Saints, on whose constant intercession in your presence we rely for unfailing help.

May this **Sacrifice** of our reconciliation, we pray, O Lord, advance the peace and salvation of all the world. Be pleased to confirm in faith and charity your pilgrim Church on earth, with your servant N. our Pope and N. our Bishop, the Order of Bishops, all the clergy, and the entire people you have gained for your own.

Listen graciously to the prayers of this family, whom you have summoned before you: in your compassion, O merciful Father, gather to yourself all your children scattered throughout the world.

To our departed brothers and sisters and to all who were pleasing to you at their passing from this life, give kind admittance to your kingdom.

There we hope to enjoy for ever the fullness of your glory through Christ our Lord, through whom you bestow on the world all that is good.

Through him, and with him, and in him, O God, almighty Father, in the unity of the Holy Spirit, all glory and honor is yours, for ever and ever. (The people acclaim: Amen.)

Eucharistic Prayer IV

We give you praise, Father most holy, for you are great and you have fashioned all your works in wisdom and in love. You formed man in your own image and entrusted the whole world to his care, so that in serving you alone, the Creator, he might have dominion over all creatures. And when through disobedience he had lost your friendship, you did not abandon him to the domain of death. For you came in mercy to the aid of all, so that those who seek might find you. Time and again you offered them covenants and through the prophets taught them to look forward to salvation.

And you so loved the world, Father most holy, that in the fullness of time you sent your Only Begotten Son to be our Savior. Made incarnate by the Holy Spirit and born of the Virgin Mary, he shared our human nature in all things but sin. To the poor he proclaimed the good news of salvation, to prisoners, freedom, and to the sorrowful of heart, joy. To accomplish your plan, he gave himself up to death, and, rising from the dead, he destroyed death and restored life.

And that we might live no longer for ourselves but for him who died and rose again for us, he sent the Holy Spirit from you, Father, as the first fruits for those who believe, so that, bringing to perfection his work in the world, he might sanctify creation to the full.

Therefore, O Lord, we pray: may this same Holy Spirit graciously sanctify these **offerings**, that they may become the

Body and Blood of our Lord Jesus Christ for the celebration of this great mystery, which he himself left us as an eternal covenant.

For when the hour had come for him to be glorified by you, Father most holy, having loved his own who were in the world, he loved them to the end: and while they were at supper, he took bread, blessed and broke it, and gave it to his disciples, saying, TAKE THIS, ALL OF YOU, AND EAT OF IT, FOR THIS IS MY BODY, WHICH WILL BE GIVEN UP FOR YOU.

In a similar way, taking the chalice filled with the fruit of the vine, he gave thanks, and gave the chalice to his disciples, saying: TAKE THIS, ALL OF YOU, AND DRINK FROM IT, FOR THIS IS THE CHALICE OF MY BLOOD, THE BLOOD OF THE NEW AND ETERNAL COVENANT, WHICH WILL BE POURED OUT FOR YOU AND FOR MANY FOR THE FORGIVENESS OF SINS. DO THIS IN MEMORY OF ME.

Therefore, O Lord, as we now celebrate the memorial of our redemption, we remember Christ's Death and his descent to the realm of the dead, we proclaim his Resurrection and his Ascension to your right hand, and, as we await his coming in glory, we offer you his Body and Blood, the **sacrifice** acceptable to you which brings salvation to the whole world.

Look, O Lord, upon the **Sacrifice** which you yourself have provided for your Church, and grant in your loving kindness to all who partake of this one Bread and one Chalice that, gathered into one body by the Holy Spirit, they may truly become a living **sacrifice** in Christ to the praise of your glory.

Therefore, Lord, remember now all for whom we offer this **sacrifice**: especially your servant N. our Pope, N. our Bishop, and the whole Order of Bishops, all the clergy, those who take part in this **offering**, those gathered here before you, your entire people, and all who seek you with a sincere heart.

Remember also those who have died in the peace of your Christ and all the dead, hose faith you alone have known.

To all of us, your children, grant, O merciful Father, that we may enter into a heavenly inheritance with the Blessed Virgin Mary, Mother of God, with blessed Joseph, her Spouse, and with your Apostles and Saints in your kingdom. There, with the whole of creation, freed from the corruption of sin and death, may we glorify you through Christ our Lord, through whom you bestow on the world all that is good.

Through him, and with him, and in him, O God, almighty Father, in the unity of the Holy Spirit, all glory and honor is yours, for ever and ever. (The people acclaim: Amen.)